GUERRILLA ADVERTISING

In one 24-hour period in 2002, a staggering 16,000 butterfly stickers, some bearing the slogan 'It's Better with the Butterfly', appeared on buildings, windows and sidewalks i
Central Park where a promotional event launching Internet software package MSN8 was taking place. Advertising in this way is illegal in New York and so, on 26 October of tha
So was this an example of a guerrilla marketing ploy gone horribly wrong? Not likely. The butterflies were Static-Cling (using static electricity as the sticking agent, not glue), s
but to a far larger audience. The campaign generated no fewer than 168 news articles around the world. This simple guerrilla campaign for France's most popular stain removing
appear as yellow boxes outside office buildings. Agency Dentsu Young & Rubicam spotted an opportunity for their client, the Singapore Cancer Society, to remind smokers of th
Safe House (WISH) is a centre in Vancouver's Downtown Eastside district that caters for women working in the sex industry. Its goal is to increase the health, safety and well-be
left this cardboard cut-out of a woman, clearly intended to look like a prostitute, tied to a lamppost on a Vancouver street. Over the course of several weeks, the cut-out was ra
woman should be left out on the streets. Support our safe house for sex workers,' along with the number on which to contact WISH. To promote World Water Day
on the body of the bins to highlight facts such as 'Polluted Water Kills 6,000 People a Day' and 'Over a Billion People Drink Worse'. Did you know that cat pee glows under blac
(rigged up as a black light) came on, glowing hand-applied lettering spelled out this curious fact, with the strapline 'We can explain.' As part of the same campaign for Science W
the fact that some 300 cases of this bizarre occurrence have been reported. Every parent who does the school run past this fun installation by Energizer in Malaysia will doubt
man. A great campaign for Amnesty International to drive home the horror that in too many places in the world people are locked up in appalling conditions simply because th
person were imprisoned beneath. Chalk 'goals' appeared on brick walls in Amsterdam during the spring of 1996, accompanied not by copy but by the familiar Nike 'swoosh'. St
their own football pitch with minimal resources. With this initiative Nike promoted the "Just do it" spirit in a simple way. This idea was executed in 1996 when it was still uncor
depicting images that were unmistakably of New York (in this case the Manhattan skyline) and which fused into something typically Tahitian. Here the illustration has been man
way. Few, however, have invested in the culture of street art as impressively as this campaign from BBDO's Johannesburg outpost. 35 huge artworks – essentially giant banners –
idea that the network was not merely rooted in the culture of the locality, but also recognized and supported it. The artworks are all still in place. This campaign was so succes
unharnessed by advertising. This campaign dates from 2000. To encourage traffic to the website britart.com, agency Mother stuck up hundreds of labels around London, targe
generating oxygen. A metaphor for life itself,' while a cashpoint was labelled an 'Interactive installation piece; theme: consumerism.' The ads recall the joke in whic
into art – from 'CD Player' to 'Badly Dressed Person'– and also art pencils, the message being that you can make anything art simply by writing or drawing on it. As part of its
billboard on the Reuters building in Times Square. Passers by were able to call a special number that was featured on the sign, and then use their mobile phone as a virtual mou
real time. Once a design was completed, the user's phone received a text message that included a link whereby they could download mobile wallpaper of their freshly designed s
put it). The text message also contained a unique PIN code and a text link that served as a gateway page into nikeid.com. By entering the code on this page, users were able to re
Nike Free 5.0 shoes to every caller over a four-hour period. To support the Nike TV campaign for Nikespeed.com, You're Faster than you Think, Publicis Mojo in Melbourne, A
obvious ailment that requires them to reach a soothing destination – fast. These character stickers were then placed near an appropriate location such as a bin (Vomit), an area
directly to the desired destination. In this seriously hard-hitting campaign, over-sized flyers were placed, image-side down, on the windscreens of cars parked near schools in
windscreen shattered by the impact of a horrifically injured child, accompanied by the simple, polite request, 'Please don't speed near schools.' 'Urban speeding is a real proble
save lives, and the combination of extremely emotive imagery – of a driver's and a parent's worst nightmare – and the calm copy gets this message across succinctly and chilling
& Saatchi. Black skid marks lead from the road, up onto pavements and straight into bus shelters, park benches or brick walls – and the words 'Drink driving ends here.' Just as a p
references in the least sporty of environments. The dangling rings for standing passengers to steady themselves on a commuter train make immediate reference to gymnastic rin
are the fruit of Indian ad agency Contract's determination to find new ways and new places to advertise for their client Fame Adlabs, a huge five-screen multiplex cinema in Mu
buoy nearby in the background happens to look like the top of a submerged skyscraper, adding to the effect. 'The spire in the background is neither photoshopped nor did w
cinema-goers
A-Rape Taxis,
be returned to
to shade the in
of small children who have stowed away inside them. Stencilled text on the back of the lorry tells us: 'Every year millions of children are trafficked for forced labour or sexua
camera. These oversized models were then left strategically in public locations where they could hardly be missed – together with a small sign with the message about the zoo
resistant coating, and filled it – apparently – with banknotes to the value of over three million Canadian dollars. In fact most of the bills were fake, with about $500 in real bills n
hours later with their families. The following morning we hit the front page of the *Vancouver Sun*. Then the news stations started showing up in earnest. We made the 5:00 news c
poster, which appeared in London late in 2004, featured a giant, three-dimensional light bulb against *The Economist* magazine's trademark red background – alluding, of course,
small sensor hidden by the bulb that detects movement [which is] triggered whenever a pedestrian walks beneath it.' When Brockwell Lido was set to close permanently in
opportunity. The logo was clearly visible from the various flight paths above London, and Cake organized a variety of events, ranging from Evian-sponsored kids' lifeguard lesso
strange pattern forms a stripe across each poster, which is otherwise white apart form a small Nike logo in the top right-hand corner. This intriguing pattern invites investigatio
of posters is designed to give the impression that a Nike trainer has ripped through all of them like a speeding bullet. These maps were created as a functional gift to runners in
and relieve themselves. To collect this information, creatives from W+K went out and scoured the city for runner-friendly rest rooms, rating them according to runner-relevant
agencies over the past couple of years. This is because rather than using paint to give form to his stencil shapes, he uses detergent to clean away the grime of the city and reveal cl
much longer than one afternoon to find suitable locations though – ie two points from which to "hang" the clothes line – two trees, two lamp posts that were situated against a
to actually apply this idea to a cleaning product. Here we see washing lines strung up on dirty walls and fences. Noticeably clean clothes. Good, appropriate use of media/mec
and also the thickness of the shakes. In the sweltering heat of August 2004 they rolled out the city's famous orange snow ploughs, emblematic of the bitter cold of winter here. T
in the image, so enhancing the illusion of an upside-down drinks carton containing a drink so thick that it doesn't simply fall out. This idea is so simple that it hardly needs exp
the ballerina pirouettes. Why? To promote the city's Joffrey Ballet School, of course. More ingenious use of unconventional media space – a great idea from JWT São Paulo's of
building into a landmark and a talking point, while staying brilliantly relevant to the product. This incredible 5.8 x 15-metre (19 x 49-foot) billboard appeared on the corner of
furniture supplied by IKEA, complete with living room, bathroom, kitchen, a working TV and computer, magazines on the coffee table and even leftover Chinese take-away foo
is a bit steep – $12,000 a month.' At around the time of this ad, Absolut was a leading player in unconventional or ambient advertising. There was a 4.3-metre (14-foot) Absolut
adjacent letters spelling out the word Absolut. In Chile in 1999, TBWA planted a field of flowers in the shape of the now iconic bottle, dubbing the piece Absolut Summer. Sinc
which shoppers could go to try freezing vodka served in glasses made of ice. Not all infants are registered at birth, particularly in remote villages. And if officially they don't ex
As people passed by they triggered the sound of a baby crying. When they leaned over to look at the baby, they found instead the disquieting information that 'Every day 136,
campaign lasted only three days before confused police started to collect up the prams. But this was not before a major newspaper had given it coverage. UNICEF collected some
Gym near Vancouver, the grocery dividers in a supermarket round the corner from the gym were lead-weighted to make them far heavier than usual, and branded with the nar
message out of the gym,' explains copywriter Bryan Collins. 'There are two ways to interpret the message from this grocery divider. It could be as simple as "Lift weights – Gol
that gets people thinking about their fitness and uses a medium in a way nobody is expecting.' Rather than succumb to the cliché of producing a TV spot for dog food showing
absolutely delicious – if you were a dog, that is. Thus it was that dogs, tails wagging, led their owners to the ads, before demonstrating that they could still do that puppy-dog ey
that the gaming environment is an interesting developing media space for brands. Launched at the end of 2003 on PS2, Xbox, Gamecube and PC, Worms 3D contains a unique
game, supply crates parachute into the landscape, each containing a potentially useful weapon, tool or health pack. This is where Red Bull comes in. The energy drink in its icon
in both attack and escape modes. So here we see Red Bull being drunk and providing health and performance benefits – exactly the kind of claims that the brand has not been
way. The game is played through Dredd's eyes as he patrols the mean streets of the futuristic metropolis MegaCity One, dealing with litterers, loiterers, junkies and worse, whi
illegally, according to Judge Dredd's harsh ban on stimulants, into the city and the player needs to keep control of suppliers handling the product in the city's docklands. Gangs
walls where 'dealers' want to attract custom. We are again dealing with branded content here, but 'product benefit' takes a more indirect form than in Worms 3D. This project s
from the brand's Spring/Summer'06 collection. But this film, on paper at least (at the time of writing it was still in post production), doesn't offer the usual kind of brand co
strategy for Meltin' Pot's communications for the season, from billboards to TV commercials, is set to revolve around the movie and its principal characters, whose wardrobes f
books were all shot by Rankin on the film set. So how did this project come about? Company director Augusto Romano originally approached Rankin, the brand's creative dire
on one written by Tony Grisoni, author of the screenplay for Terry Gilliam's *Fear and Loathing in Las Vegas*. Seattle's Science Fiction Museum and Hall of Fame was opened in 2004 to
what the genre tends to do: blur the lines between fact and fiction. The ads they created teased Seattle with campaigns promoting futuristic products and services, but set in co
ship ready for take off against the backdrop of the Seattle skyline boasted the headline: 'Elliott Bay Lunar Vacations. Leave your troubles 240,000 miles behind!' The campaign
retail outlets included 'Intergalactic Alien Pet Imports', Seattle's largest supplier of 12-eyed sycophish, shipped daily from Epsilon Prime. Two footballers, suspended high abov
stunt that proved impossible to ignore: traffic came to a standstill as people stopped to check out the action and take photographs. The stunt received coverage on local and int
with this campaign, It's Raining Men. And that's exactly what happened. A whopping 10,000 near-naked Ken dolls (as in Barbie) were attached to carefully filledhelium balloons
a radio promotion and also with one of the bachelors featured in Cleo. Bemused and amused women caught the dolls to check them out – but did this campaign work? Reader

, the work of guerrilla marketing specialists OutdoorVision/ALT TERRAIN LLC. The butterflies formed a trail leading from Times Square, where MSN had a major billboard, through to
onse to a major public and municipal outcry against the campaign, Microsoft formally apologized to the city of New York and agreed to stop the campaign and help the city clean it up.
were very easy to remove and left no residue. By bending a few rules and ruffling more than a few feathers, Microsoft had communicated not just to people on the streets of Manhattan
r, involved finding stains on pavements or streets and creating white, clothes-shaped outlines around them, with the simple line: 'Try K2r'. In Singapore, designated smoking areas often
cts of their stinky habit. Thus coffin-shaped yellow boxes were painted all over the city, bearing the message 'Designated Smokers' Area'. Simple but poignant. The Women's Information
en working in the sex trade in Vancouver and support women when they choose to exit that particular lifestyle. To raise awareness of the charitable organization's cause, agency Rethink
shed with dirt from the road, and generally abused by both the elements and passers by. When it looked bedraggled and thoroughly wrecked, Rethink added a sign with the copy: 'No
bish bins in Sydney were dressed with appropriately proportioned straws, handles and even lemon slices to make them resemble drinking cups. Various messages appeared
dian agency Rethink put this fact to the test in a bus shelter Adshel for client Science World: the resulting ad appeared as just a white poster by day; but by night, when the Adshel's light
k left the supposed remains of a case of spontaneous human combustion – including a pile of ashes, a pair of shoes, the cuff of a shirt and a walking stick – in front of an ad spelling out
trouble with the little ones should they return from the shops with the 'wrong' brand of battery. Not so much an ad as a landmark, there's just no way you could miss this jolly battery
beliefs, skin colour or opinions differ from those of the regime under which they live. The campaign consisted of pairs of model hands gripping the grille of street drains – as though a
or Matthijs de Jongh of Dutch agency KesselsKramer explains the logic of the campaign: 'By drawing goals with chalk Nike wanted to inspire kids in the suburbs of Amsterdam to create
k in media other than posters, print ads or commercials.' To advertise flights from NYC to Tahiti, Saatchi & Saatchi commissioned illustrator Dennis Clouse to create single-line drawings
metal and mounted on a brick wall. Many agencies and brands around the world have used graffiti methods such as stencilling to bring their campaigns on to the street in an engaging
et' artists were erected on the sides of buildings in downtown Johannesburg in 2003 to promote the mobile phone network Cell C. Entitled For The City, the project demonstrated the
#work set up a new branch in Johannesburg called New#tork in order to produce work with a specifically African flavour, drawing on local street culture of arts and crafts previously
yday objects that make up the fabric of urban life. Each label identified the object in question in artspeak, as if it were an exhibit in a gallery. Thus a tree became an 'Organic sculpture
guard's chair is mistaken for an exhibit, while also reminding us that art is indeed all around us. Mother also produced 'artalizers', or stickers to turn whatever you want
for the relaunch of nikeid.com – the site that enables consumers to custom-design trainers – agency R/GA created this interactive experience, mounted on the huge 23-storey digital
a design of the Nike Free 5.0 trainer, using a modified palette of colours. As participants pressed buttons on their phones, so the colours on the on-screen image of the shoe changed in
e with a Times Square message to serve as a souvenir of the experience (this was after all 'the world's first cellphone-controlled, commerce-enabled interactive experience', as the agency
imes Square creation with the option to further customize the shoe, and then actually to buy it. On the last day of the campaign Nike hosted a 'Friday Free For All', when they gave away
missioned two local street artists to create graphics showing characters needing to get somewhere fast. Artists Regular Product and Cailan both produced two characters, each with an
s), a toilet (Curry Man), or a drinking fountain (Chilli). The stickers all incorporate a long arrow, with the words 'You're Faster than you Think' running along the length of it, pointing
region of New Zealand. Drivers returning to their cars would see only the white back of the flyer until they climbed inside – at which point they were confronted with the sight of a
own New Zealand,' explains Toby Talbot, 'and some of the biggest culprits, ironically, are parents who rush to drop their kids at school each morning.' Simply reducing speed really does
roads are becoming increasingly safe – the reason, according to road safety researchers, being mainly due to the good response to drink-driving campaigns such as this one from Saatchi
st for Christmas, Adidas's 'Forever Sport' campaign was designed to let consumers know that sport is ever-present – no matter where they are or what the occasion. Hence these sporting
slapping the brand's logo and the campaign's strapline next to them. Similarly, metal railings make reference to parallel bars with the aid of an adjacent campaign sticker. These two ads
Indian cinema release of the global disaster movie *The Day After Tomorrow*, they placed a billboard in the sea, just off the beach, with the title and release date visible above the waterline. A
,' explains creative director Ashutosh Karkhanis. 'It has always been there. It's a post to which fishermen tie their boats.' To promote the release of *Spiderman* 2 in India, meanwhile, male
s such as Risk-
perators could
reens designed
uddled figures
'. Normally small objects, such as leaves and swimming pool armbands, were literally made ten times bigger to demonstrate the 10X optical zoom power offered by a new Olympus
the Olympus C-740 Ultrazoom camera. To promote the security glass produced by a local company, Canadian agency Rethink ingeniously treated a bus shelter's Adshel with a shatter-
top layer. 'The reaction was extraordinary,' recalls copywriter Bryan Collins. 'Almost everyone who walked by ended up kicking, punching and body-checking the glass. People returned
on and nationally on several networks. Since then, the story has run in countless newspapers and magazines around the world. All this for a $6,000 CDN investment.' This special-build
t brains of those who read it. The bulb lit up every time someone passed directly beneath it, as Paul Belford explains: 'It actually works on the same principle as security lights. There's a
client Evian stepped in to sponsor it, matching owner Lambeth Council's £100,000 investment that year to improve it and keep it open – and of course to make it a huge branding
arty with Basement Jaxx headlining. Anyone walking past this row of six Adshels taken over by Nike in Singapore might have wondered what exactly the sports brand was advertising. A
n you see the final Adshel on the far right of the series, and notice the front of a trainer looking as though it's bursting through the actual structure of it, does it become clear that the set
Marathon in 2003. All urban runners will know the importance of having a good place to use as a pit stop, so the maps helpfully point out a selection of places where runners can stop
even photographed them. The end result may look confusing to the untrained eye – but not, we're assured, to runners. Graffiti artist Moose has been much in demand from advertising
n dirty walls or pavements. 'This campaign was all done in one afternoon and these images were all taken around Abbey Road and Belsize Road in North London,' reveals Moose.' It took
would respond to my cleaning methods.' The beauty of this campaign is that cleaning walls isn't illegal or defacing. It was only a matter of time before a bright spark at an agency thought
enturous stuff for Procter & Gamble. To launch McDonald's Arctic Orange Triple Thick milkshakes in Chicago, Leo Burnett came up with two local campaigns to underline the coldness
riple Thick campaign, they cleverly used a billboard to boast of the thickness of the drink. The post that supports the billboard was adorned with a stripe that perfectly matched the straw
w York's Saatchi & Saatchi office came up with this clever use of a revolving door as the animation tool that makes a life-size image of a ballerina actually dance: when the door revolves,
Food's Royal baking powder: taking over two huge walls of this bizarre-shaped building and make it look as if it's a cross-section of a massive cake. This campaign instantly turned the
l Bond Street in New York in the summer of 2000, and stayed there for the rest of the year. The billboard showed a life-size studio flat in the shape of an Absolut vodka bottle, filled with
t's] a pretty good-size apartment,' observed Richard Lewis, then worldwide account director on the brand for TBWA\Chiat\Day, New York. 'Actually it's a great place to live, but the rent
nset Boulevard, and another on a suburban highway in Miami, the latter being part of an ongoing performance piece involving painting the bottle with a thousand layers of paint, with
K has seen executions for the brand such as Absolut Zero, a bottle-shaped ice rink, and Absolut Chilled, a bottle-shaped igloo built of ice outside a shopping centre in Manchester, into
may be easy victims of child abuse. To promote a campaign by UNICEF to raise awareness of this issue, agency åkestam.holst left a number of empty prams in the streets of Stockholm.
are born who do not exist', accompanied by a voiceover calling for support for the child registration campaign. Though it created a powerful metaphor for non-existent children, this
World Parents' who give monetary support on a regular basis – in the immediate aftermath of the campaign. In this entertaining local campaign by agency Rethink for a branch of Gold's
n. The result was that most shoppers struggled to pick them up and move them – so highlighting the potential to tone up those biceps. 'The idea here is simply to try and take the gym's
t what we really wanted was for people to have that moment where they can't lift something they really should be able to, and think: "Man, I need to get to the gym". It's a funny prank
oh-so-glossy Labrador leaping blithely around a sunny park (in slow motion), Michael Conrad & Leo Burnett in Frankfurt produced these dog-height posters that were treated to smell
h of course is the doggy equivalent of emotional blackmail... Can't think of a better ad for dog food. Experiential and very definitely unconventional, these two campaigns demonstrate
of writing) piece of branded content. Players control teams of heavily armed Worms, ensuring they blow the stuffing out of each other using a huge variety of weapons. Throughout the
lver can appears in the game as one of the available 'power-ups'. When a player selects a can of Red Bull, their health value is boosted by up to 100 per cent and they become much faster
ake in its TV campaigns. Launched about the same time as Worms 3D in late 2003, Judge Dredd: Dredd vs Death sees the inclusion of Red Bull in the gaming environment in a different
g to save the city from the evil Judge Death. In order to keep the populace in check, stimulants such as caffeine are controlled substances. Step in Red Bull. The drink is being smuggled
lealers' are notably more agile, better shots and altogether harder to subdue than other characters in the game. Red Bull logos appear on crates, and glowing graffiti logos are 'tagged' on
ns brand Meltin' Pot hook up with photographer, publisher and now director Rankin to create a feature-length film. Ostensibly an exercise in branded content, the film features clothes
es of the Saints is a real film, with a good script and a plot that leans towards magical realism, offering an engaging alternative to the catwalk parade favoured by most fashion brands. The
from the season's collection. So while posters and trailers for the film will promote a promising piece of cinema, viewers will be exposed to the brand's new collection. The season's look
a short film. Rankin's response was to embark on an extensive search for a full-length script (aided by a script competition held through *Dazed and Confused* magazine), eventually settling
to the genre, with displays ranging from Captain James T. Kirk's command chair to costumes from *Planet of the Apes*. To publicize the museum, Cole & Weber/Red Cell decided to do exactly
Seattle landscapes. Postcards promoting Seattle Transit's new 'Hover Bus' displayed a photo of a Seattle street complete with a futuristic hovering bus, while poster ads showing a rocket
posters placed in empty store fronts to advertise the business that was supposedly about to open on the premises, complete with logos and lists of services available. Eye-catching new
treets, play a death-defying game as they attempt to score goals past each other, kicking a football, also suspended on a rope, against the back-drop of a huge green billboard. This was a
ews channels. Australian women's magazine *Cleo* briefed agency Maverick to encourage their readership to vote in their Bachelor of the Year promotion in April 2002. Maverick came up
descended gently) and dropped over the beaches and shopping areas of Melbourne and Sydney. The dolls were dressed only in white boxer shorts, and each bore a tag linking him with
agazine increased 12 per cent over the previous issue, while there was an 8 per cent response to the voting numbers attached to the dolls. And of course the sight of several thousand Ken

GUERRILLA

UNCONVENTIONAL BRAND COMMUNICATION

ADVERTIS-ING

Written by Gavin Lucas
Art Direction by Michael Dorrian

THANK YOU

Published in 2006 by
Laurence King Publishing Ltd
71 Great Russell Street
London WC1B 3BP
United Kingdom

Tel: +44 20 7430 8850
Fax: +44 20 7430 8880
e-mail: enquiries@laurenceking.co.uk
www.laurenceking.co.uk

A catalogue record for this book is
available from the British Library

ISBN-13 978-185669-470-4
ISBN-10 1-85669-470-4

WORDS Gavin Lucas

ART DIRECTION Michael Dorrian,
Tony Fox, James Sterling

DESIGN AND LAYOUT Tony Fox,
James Sterling

PAGE 1 symbolix.com

PAGE 1 PHOTOGRAPHY
Jim@jimfenwick.com

PRINTED IN CHINA

Ty Montague, Moose, Jo Lightfoot, Emily Asquith, Andy Prince, Mark
Sinclair, Nathan Gale, Patrick Burgoyne, Paula Carson, Phil Dowgierd,
Brad Fairhead, Steve Turner, Jeremy Craigen, Peter and Angela Lucas,
Ami Brophy, Dov Schiff, Jeani Rodgers, Kati Holloway, Ruth Harlow,
Annouchka Behrmann, Ellie Mooney, Sarah Farmer, Sabine Gilhuijs,
Michelle Lim, Angus Macadam, Andrew McGovern, Orna Malone,
Adam Salacuse, Sarah Park, David Nobay, Jonathan Hawkins, Jim
Fenwick, Grant Hunter, Jakob Berndt, Selena McKenzie, Adam
Cruickshank, Hugh Todd, Bronwen Diviani, James Lee Duffy, Grace
Yong, Lauren Freeman, Cass Davidson, Shane Gibson, Philip Slade,
John Merrifield, Jim Hilson, Helen Kimber, Katrin Kester, Natalie
Brown, Felicitas Ronnimois, Louise Drewett, Franziska Danger, Din
Sumedi, Laurence Quinn, Marie Neo, Martin Muir, Mike Curtis,
Darren Whittingham, Fred Deakin, Nat Hunter, Kerrie Finch, Dave
Cobban, Millie Munro and Joe Wade.

Special thanks to our families and in particular Ravi and Cessie
for all their encouragement and invaluable assistance.

LAURENCE KING

CONTENTS

STREET PROPAGANDA

22 It's Better with the Butterfly
26 Try K2r
28 Smoke Box
29 Cutout
30 Bins
32 Cat Pee/Spontaneous Combustion
34 Monorail
36 Wrong Colour/Wrong Opinion/
   Wrong Faith
38 Goals
40 Skyline
42 For the City
44 Britart
46 Nike iD Reuters Sign

SITE-SPECIFIC MEDIA

50 You're Faster than you Think
54 Windscreen Flyer
56 Drink Driving Ends Here
58 Parallel Bars/Rings
60 Submerged Hoarding/Loo
62 Cab Cards
63 Smart – Surprisingly Spacious
64 Save the Children Lorry
66 Floats/Leaves
68 Money
70 Light Bulb
72 Evian Lido
74 Nike Speed
76 Nature Calls Map
78 Graffiti
80 Snow Plough/Triple Thick
82 Ballerina
83 Really, Really Big Cake
84 Absolut New York

SNEAKY MANOEUVRES

88 Pram
90 Grocery Divider
91 Smelling Billboard
92 Worms 3D/Judge Dredd: Dredd vs
    Death
94 The Lives of the Saints
96 Science Fiction Launch Campaign

STUNTS

104 Vertical Football
106 It's Raining Men
108 The World's First Inflatable Church
112 Homesick?
114 Red Carpet
116 CSI: Locker/Beach/Trunk/Toilet
120 London is Closer than you Think
122 Departure Lounge
126 Toy Box
127 Taxi Launderette
128 Ice Polo
129 Eggs
130 Radar Van
132 Missile Car
134 Driverless Delivery Van
136 Impossible Bus Pull
138 Make Trade Fair
140 Singing Tower
144 The Ass of Commons
146 Digital Aquarium
150 Go Cubic
152 Be Proud of your Loo
153 Move It
154 Impossible Sprint
156 Bed

MULTI-FRONTED ATTACK

160 Beta-7
166 HYPE
174 Remember Rainier
180 Subservient Chicken
184 Chicken Fight

I spend a lot of time these days groping around for appropriate metaphors to describe the time we find ourselves in today in the advertising business. My current favourite: the transatlantic shipping business in the early 20th century.

This was an age dominated by great brands like Cunard and Whitestar. At their height, these companies employed state of the art technology – big, fast, beautiful ships – and catered not only for the common folk, but also for the social élite: the Astors, the Morgans, the Carnegies. It was a romantic time, a time full of possibility. And if you had asked the people at Cunard and Whitestar what business they were in they would, in all likelihood, have answered with some justifiable pride, the transatlantic shipping business.

They would also have been quite wrong. It transpired they were not in the transatlantic shipping business, but rather the transatlantic people-moving business. Small semantic distinction? Nope. Life or death issue. Because it became clear that people didn't want to cross the Atlantic Ocean in ships. They wanted to cross the Atlantic Ocean as fast as possible. We all know how it turned out – a new technology, the airplane, came along and people embraced it in droves. The transatlantic people-moving business continued to grow rapidly for the rest of the century. But the great brands of the previous era, the Cunards and Whitestars, did not make the leap with them. The transatlantic shipping business sank without a ripple.

So, whatever your vocation, figuring out what business you are really in is fairly important. Especially if you find yourself, as I do, sitting on the bridge of a venerable old advertising ship like JWT at the dawn of what I believe is literally a new age in communication.

If you were to ask the same question, 'what business are you in?' at most agencies today, my guess is that by far the most common answer would be 'the advertising business'. Understandable and, in my opinion, also completely wrong. If we continue to define ourselves as an industry as being in 'advertising', my belief is we're pretty much doomed. The advertising business – the business of interrupting what people are interested in with a commercial message about something they're not interested in – is a business that is already in decline. You cannot open a paper today without reading about another major marketer reducing their TV budget. The broadcast television economy, of which 'advertising' is a significant player, is withering.

The good news: there is a new business being born simultaneously, literally all around us. Call it engagement, interactivity, participation… the fact is that it doesn't really have a satisfactory name yet. That will probably come later. But it is being born, much in the same way aviation was born. Small groups of people, working in isolation from one another and often employing untested new technologies, are creating new ways of telling stories. The Wilbur and Orville Wrights of our time are out there experimenting, trying, sometimes failing, sometimes succeeding, but pressing forward.

This book is a collection of those early experiments. They are the prototypes of the new era, and 50 years from now some of them will hang, as the Wright flyer does, in a museum and people will walk past and shake their heads and marvel at the crudeness of them. Others will stand and wonder if even the Wrights knew just how fast everything was about to change… of the amazing inventions that were to follow.

Here's the really exciting part. The invention is just beginning. The new leaders and legends of this incredible time have yet to be recognized. We have not found our Wrights, our Lindberghs, our Yeagers, our Armstrongs. Who will they be?

You, perhaps? Read on and be inspired.

TY MONTAGUE, CO-PRESIDENT, CHIEF CREATIVE OFFICER, JWT NEW YORK

INTRO
DUC-
TION

Whosoever desires
constant success must
change his conduct
with the times.

NICCOLÒ DEI MACHIAVELLI, *THE PRINCE*, 1513

Since mankind began trading goods, the advertising of a product or service has been key to creating a successful business. From the market stallholder calling out their wares to the biggest budget television commercial, customers need to know about what is on offer. Nowadays the whole world is a market place. There are millions of brands and products vying for our attention: each of us is exposed to around 1,500 brand messages a day.

Advertising is not just what we see on television, on billboards and in magazines. These are, however, the traditional and classical media channels for advertising. In the latter half of the twentieth century, television became the favoured channel for mass producers of goods to beam their brand messages through to the masses. Consequently, a formula for advertising duly emerged: the 30-second television spot, backed up by supporting press and poster advertisements. As advertising agencies grew, they developed structures, hierarchies and procedures to replicate this advertising formula, smoothly and efficiently, ad infinitum. Any other form of brand communication has traditionally been the property of media, public relations (PR) and marketing agencies.

But the landscape has changed. The number of brands on the shelves in our supermarkets has increased around 14-fold in the last 20 years. And of course we no longer have just a handful of television channels, each guaranteeing massive viewing figures for advertisers. There are now umpteen television channels for consumers to choose from, and so the television audience is increasingly fragmented. Add to this the arrival of technologies such as Personal Video Recorders (PVRs), with which consumers can effectively screen out television advertising, not to mention ever more sophisticated hand-held communication gadgets, and advertising agencies are left with no choice but to investigate alternative channels of communication.

Consumers are now very much in control of the media they consume and how they consume it, so advertisers can no longer spoon-feed messages to the masses in television ad breaks as they once did. Advertisers and agencies have had to take note and evolve, both with the rapidly changing media landscape around them and with the changing habits of consumers, in order to explore the options beyond television, press and poster.

Branded content and sponsorship deals, trend and youth marketing, outdoor or ambient-style campaigns that look to catch consumers off their guard – the list of communications options keeps on growing. Rather than produce a poster or a press or television campaign, a brand might fly a hot-air balloon around the world; record and distribute a music track; throw a party in a park; produce content that can travel virally via email; sponsor a club night; create a magazine, television show or film; or devise interactive games or services that can be accessed through cellular phones or the Internet.

The advancement of technology is as much a factor in these new options as agencies' increasing bravery in terms of thinking and acting outside the constraints of traditional advertising. Now you can create an animated poster using lenticular technology. A film distributor might place inexpensive screens in street-level Adshels, triggered by sensors so that when someone passes by, a movie star winks at them, enticing them to watch their latest movie trailer by pressing a button. Or you could take advantage of infrared technology and invite consumers to use a transmitting tag, embedded in a poster to download information to their phone. Hypertag, a company specializing in this technology, produced the campaign for New Order's 2005 album *Waiting for the Siren's Call*, in which people passing HMV music shop windows could download an MP3 track from the album simply by pointing their phone to a specific area of the window. In 1999, mobile phone firm Ericsson unveiled Bluetooth, another technology that allows information to be beamed to consumers' mobile phones or Personal Digital Assistants (PDAs).

This is not to suggest that promotional activities which take advantage of such non-traditional advertising media channels are recent contrivances. On the contrary, marketing and PR companies have long championed the publicity stunt or public event as a method of getting their client's product talked about, just as media companies have been devising non-traditional, yet appropriate, media channel activities for brands to implement as part of their marketing.

What is now happening, however, is that advertising agencies are becoming aware of the need to keep up with what these other companies offer, as they see television beginning to take its place on a level playing field of media options. Big global advertising agencies are now capable of producing campaigns that are rooted in the traditions of their PR and media company cousins rather than in those of classical ad agency output. TBWA\Japan's Impossible Sprint (see pages 154–5) and Vertical Football (pages 104–5) campaigns for Adidas are good examples of this shift towards unconventional approaches by advertising agencies. Another example can be found in Wieden + Kennedy's Portland office's development of a project called Ball, a Broadway musical about basketball, wholly funded by Nike.

Advertising is changing. Advertising agencies that fail to embrace this change, evolve and develop are in danger, in true Darwinian style, of becoming extinct. Some major advertising networks have already begun to restructure accordingly, and are setting up departments that can produce non-classical advertising. Wieden + Kennedy London have set up Fat; Lowe Worldwide has their Activation department; Saatchi & Saatchi has Saatchi & SaatchiX; and Fallon in London has set up Happen.

So what exactly is going on in these new departments? 'Fallon's investment in what Happen are doing', explains Happen partner Phil Dowgierd, 'is Fallon's response to the need for a function that can support a creative idea that is not an advertisement [in the traditional sense], and be able to work out a way to execute it. [The agency] is trying to move away from having a vested interest in just one channel or one set of channels.' Dowgierd's colleague

Brad Fairhead goes on: 'What we're trying to do is to plug consumer insight at the front end of the creative process, so that it is not just about the brand but about the consumer of that brand too, in order to understand how to connect to them and what they're interested in. [The agency has to discover] where to engage effectively with them and then, when you've got all those different insights, the big idea will stand alone. From that process comes different articulations. It is not about matching luggage, it is more about an idea that is expressed in different ways, which is true to an overriding theme.'

Rather than starting with the thought that a communication will inevitably be in the form of a television spot and then working backwards to shoehorn an idea into that format, these forward-thinking agency departments look to develop brand-relevant ideas first. At the same time they nurture an impartial approach towards media channels, so ensuring that each campaign appropriates the media channel most naturally suited to it.

In response to this changing approach to advertising, the Clio international advertising awards introduced a new category in 2004. Content & Contact was set up to give recognition to campaigns beyond the realm of television – campaigns that are innovative in terms of the way they communicate, and successful in communicating to a targeted and appropriate audience. 'I invented the category', explains Clio awards director Ami Brophy, 'because the most exciting leading agencies were focusing their efforts on projects that included creatives and also media strategists at the same time.'

The first campaign to take the grand prix in the Content & Contact category at the 2004 Clios was Beta-7 by Wieden + Kennedy New York, for Sega's American football game, ESPN NFL. This campaign (see pages 160–165) made clever use of the Internet and blog culture to infiltrate the gaming community, and in doing so to confuse, intrigue and engage them far more than a television advert ever could. Ad spend on this campaign was far from traditional.

An actor was employed for four months to play the role of Beta-7, and the campaign unfolded over the Internet in all its complexity over that period. During this time the actor was in character 24 hours a day, available to respond to emails and participate in live blogs online. Beta-7 was an ingeniously original and effective campaign, and its win of the Clios' new category seemed to mark the dawn of a new era in advertising.

BMW's win the previous year at the industry's Cannes awards, in a new category set up to recognize innovation in advertising, also heralded a new era. Their series of short films, The Hire, was essentially an exercise in branded content (albeit on a grand scale never produced by a single brand before), but it had something in common with W+K's Beta-7. Here was brand-funded content that engaged consumers, intriguing them until they were hooked. This was material that consumers actively wanted to seek out, absorb and discuss. This triggered response flies in the face of PVR technology and a recent example was Crispin Porter & Bogusky in Miami's viral campaign for Burger King (see pages 180–83). Here, a link to the Subservient Chicken site was sent to 30 people, who in turn passed it on to more and more friends. A week later the site had been visited by thousands of people all over the world. The campaign was not just about getting consumers to buy a burger: it was about making them laugh, impressing them with its irreverence and persuading them that the site was good enough to forward to others: a brilliantly successful campaign strategy that cost a fraction of the price of broadcasting on television.

Television, billboard and press advertisements are expensive to implement and yet, for the most part, they have become background noise in the life of today's consumers, assailed as we are by hundreds of brand messages from a growing variety of sources. This is not to say that traditional advertising will die. On the contrary, the guerrilla approach, and other non-traditional methods, can offer inspiration and new vitality to classical forms, so that the two can happily sit side by side. As Phil Dowgierd of Happen notes, 'Brands like Honda have taken their television advertising to

new levels of engagement and entertainment. Engagement is a key word: advertisers have to find ways to engage their audience. If they don't, then their audience will switch off or screen out that communication.' Jeremy Craigen, executive creative director at agency DDB London agrees: 'I don't think the death of the 30-second [television] spot is imminent. The bad 30-second commercial is dead... Having 400 television channels means that whatever we do has to be more effective. You want everyone to talk about your ad.' Good advertising agencies are bound to rise not just to the challenge of the extension in the number of television channels, but also to the demand to take on exciting new styles of non-traditional advertising.

'Guerrilla' is perhaps a surprising word to use as a blanket term for these new non-traditional advertising campaigns – especially as terms such as 'ambient', 'outdoor', 'disruptive' and 'integrated' seem to have more currency among the advertising fraternity. But the notion of a guerrilla campaign encapsulates the idea that this kind of advertising exists outside the normal rules of engagement, and works by seizing and subverting people's attention when and where they least expect it, and holding them captive until they have absorbed the message. In the words of Jay Conrad Levinson, who coined the term 'guerrilla marketing': 'Guerrilla marketing is more about matching wits than matching budgets. Guerrilla marketing can be as different from traditional marketing as guerrilla warfare is from traditional warfare. Rather than marching their marketing dollars forth like infantry divisions, guerrilla marketers snipe away with their marketing resources for maximum impact.'

Advertisers are currently waging war against each other, competing for attention on our streets, via our PCs and even through our mobile phone handsets and PDAs. They will stop at nothing to engage, enrage or entertain us. We MUST be talking about their brand or product. Have you seen the campaign where Adidas suspended two footballers high above a busy Tokyo square to play a death-defying game of football? Or when Sega attempted to deceive the global gaming community? What about Microsoft covering the buildings and sidewalks of Manhattan with thousands of illegal stickers overnight? There are now so many different ways in which a brand can approach its consumers that it is sometimes difficult to know when it is happening. Advertising used to be a predictable one-way communication conducted in a handful of obvious venues. Not anymore. Now, originality of voice, appropriateness of media channel and the intriguing nature of content conspire to invite the consumer to become involved in something relatively new between advertiser and consumer: a conversation.

The aim of this book is to showcase a selection of campaigns from around the world, all of which communicate by being different, by engaging the public in ways with which we are unfamiliar, using means that are strikingly appropriate to the product or service being advertised. Sometimes it is obvious what is being marketed; sometimes we are completely unaware that we are looking at, or engaging with, an advert. It is not the intention here to address ethical issues, yet there are questions of morality that such material and its manner of presentation could invite us to consider. Should advertisers be allowed to use unmonitored persuasive tactics? While there are bodies to police television and print advertising, is anyone policing these non-traditional communications? And if not, should they be?

The campaigns collected in these pages have all been implemented outside the predictable advertising media channels and were therefore (we may assume) 'unpoliced' according to established norms and criteria. I leave any moral questions to be debated elsewhere, and here celebrate what the campaigns themselves represent: a bright new era for creativity in the realm of advertising.

Opportunity in the classical media is becoming more and more challenged for a number of reasons. First, there is the cost issue. Second, the fragmentation of the media; and third, related to that, the growth of new technologies. The central challenge: to continue to differentiate products and services in an even stronger and more creative and constructive way.

MARTIN SORRELL, CHIEF EXECUTIVE OFFICER, WPP, SPEAKING AT A BRAINSTORMING SESSION ENTITLED 'BUILDING A BETTER MOUSETRAP', CANNES LIONS 2005

STREET
PROPA
GANDA

STREET PROPAGANDA   20-47

TITLE
It's Better with the Butterfly

CLIENT
Microsoft MSN8

AGENCY
Universal McCann, USA

In one 24-hour period in 2002, a staggering 16,000 butterfly stickers, some bearing the slogan 'It's Better with the Butterfly', appeared on buildings, windows and sidewalks in Manhattan, the work of guerrilla marketing specialists OutdoorVision/ ALT TERRAIN LLC. The butterflies formed a trail leading from Times Square, where MSN had a major billboard, through to Central Park where a promotional event launching Internet software package MSN8 was taking place.

Advertising in this way is illegal in New York and so, on 26 October of that year, in response to a major public and municipal outcry against the campaign, Microsoft formally apologized to the city of New York and agreed to stop the campaign and help the city to clean it up. So was this an example of a guerrilla marketing ploy gone horribly wrong? Not likely. The butterflies were Static-Cling (using static electricity as the sticking agent, not glue), so the decals were very easy to remove and left no residue. By bending a few rules and ruffling more than a few feathers, Microsoft had communicated not just to people on the streets of Manhattan, but to a far larger audience. The campaign generated no fewer than 168 news articles around the world.

MEDIA AGENCY
OutdoorVision

PRODUCTION AND IMPLEMENTATION COMPANY
ALT TERRAIN LLC

LOCATION
New York, USA

I think there are a lot of corporations that don't know that placing these ads on the sidewalks or on our pedestrian indicators – our walk/don't walk signs – is indeed illegal.

TOM COCOLA, SPOKESPERSON, NEW YORK CITY'S DEPARTMENT OF TRANSPORTATION.

This is nothing more than corporate graffiti. It's no better than all those kids out there tagging subway cars.

VANESSA GRUEN, DIRECTOR, SPECIAL PROJECTS FOR THE MUNICIPAL ART SOCIETY (A CIVIC ORGANIZATION THAT HAS LONG BATTLED THE COMMERCIALIZATION OF PUBLIC SPACE)

We apologize to the City of New York and the people of
New York City. We made a mistake with the decals, and we
take full responsibility for what happened. We are working
with city officials to clean up the decals immediately.

YUSUF MEHDI, CORPORATE VICE PRESIDENT, MSN PERSONAL SERVICES AND BUSINESS

TITLE
Try K2r

CLIENT
K2r

AGENCY
TBWA\Paris

This simple guerrilla campaign for France's most popular stain removing product, K2r, involved finding stains on pavements or streets and creating white, clothes-shaped outlines around them, with the simple line: 'Try K2r'.

CREATIVE DIRECTOR
Erik Vervroegen

ART DIRECTORS
Chris Garbutt, Matthew Branning, Eve Roussou

COPYWRITERS
Chris Garbutt, Matthew Branning

PHOTOGRAPHER
Eve Roussou

LOCATION
Paris, France

TITLE
Smoke Box

CLIENT
Singapore Cancer Society

AGENCY
Dentsu Young & Rubicam

In Singapore, designated smoking areas often appear as yellow boxes outside office buildings. Agency Dentsu Young & Rubicam spotted an opportunity for their client, the Singapore Cancer Society, to remind smokers of the deadly effects of their stinky habit. Thus coffin-shaped yellow boxes were painted all over the city, bearing the message 'Designated Smokers' Area'. Simple but poignant.

CREATIVE DIRECTORS
Mark Fong, Patrick Low

ART DIRECTOR
Kenny Choo

COPYWRITERS
Andrew Lok, Alvin Wong

PHOTOGRAPHER
Edward Loh

LOCATION
Singapore

NO WOMAN
SHOULD BE LEFT OUT
ON THE STREETS.

SUPPORT OUR SAFE HOUSE FOR SEX WORKERS. WISH

TITLE
Cutout

CLIENT
WISH Women's Shelter

AGENCY
Rethink

The Women's Information Safe House
(WISH) is a centre in Vancouver's
Downtown Eastside district that caters
for women working in the sex industry.
Its goal is to increase the health, safety
and well-being of women working in
the sex trade in Vancouver and support
women when they choose to exit that
particular lifestyle.

To raise awareness of the charitable
organization's cause, agency Rethink
left this cardboard cut-out of a woman,
clearly intended to look like a prostitute,
tied to a lamppost on a Vancouver street.
Over the course of several weeks, the
cut-out was rained on, splashed with
dirt from the road, and generally
abused by both the elements and
passers by. When it looked bedraggled
and thoroughly wrecked, Rethink added
a sign with the copy: 'No woman should
be left out on the streets. Support our
safe house for sex workers,' along with
the number on which to contact WISH.

CREATIVE DIRECTORS
Ian Grais, Chris Staples

ART DIRECTOR
Hylton Mann

COPYWRITER
Heather Vincent

PHOTOGRAPHER
Hans Sipma

LOCATION
Vancouver, Canada

To promote World Water Day public rubbish bins in
Sydney were dressed with appropriately proportioned
straws, handles and even lemon slices to make them
resemble drinking cups. Various messages appeared
on the body of the bins to highlight facts such
as 'Polluted Water Kills 6,000 People a Day' and 'Over
a Billion People Drink Worse'.

TITLE
Bins

CLIENT
United Nations

AGENCY
Saatchi & Saatchi,
Sydney

CREATIVE DIRECTOR
David Nobay

ART DIRECTOR
Vince Lagana

COPYWRITER
Luke Chess

LOCATION
Sydney, Australia

TITLE
Cat Pee/Spontaneous Combustion
CLIENT
Science World
AGENCY
Rethink

CREATIVE DIRECTORS
Ian Grais, Chris Staples

CREATIVES
Rob Sweetman,
Rob Tarry

PHOTOGRAPHER
Alastair Bird

LOCATION
Vancouver, Canada

Did you know that cat pee glows under black light? Canadian agency Rethink put this fact to the test in a bus shelter Adshel for client Science World: the resulting ad appeared as just a white poster by day; but by night, when the Adshel's light (rigged up as a black light) came on, glowing hand-applied lettering spelled out this curious fact, with the strapline 'We can explain'. As part of the same campaign for Science World, Rethink left the supposed remains of a case of spontaneous human combustion – including a pile of ashes, a pair of shoes, the cuff of a shirt and a walking stick – in front of an ad spelling out the fact that some 300 cases of this bizarre occurrence have been reported.

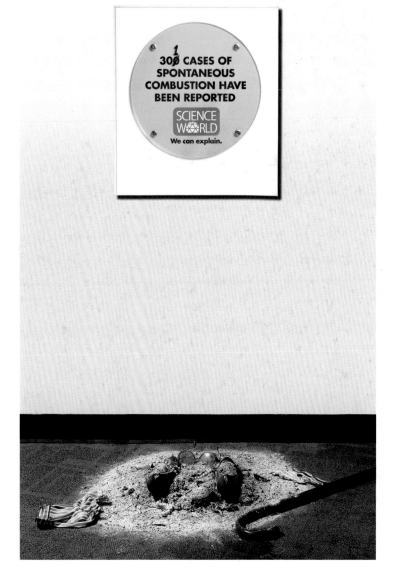

TITLE
Monorail

CLIENT
Energizer

AGENCY
Naga DDB

Every parent who does the school run past this fun installation by Energizer in Malaysia will doubtless be in big trouble with the little ones should they return from the shops with the 'wrong' brand of battery. Not so much an ad as a landmark, there's just no way you could miss this jolly battery man.

CREATIVE DIRECTOR
Ted Lim

ART DIRECTOR
Yip Chee Keong

COPYWRITER
Kay Chin

LOCATION
Kuala Lumpur, Malaysia

TITLE
Wrong Colour/Wrong
Opinion/Wrong Faith
CLIENT
Amnesty International
AGENCY
Michael Conrad & Leo Burnett

CREATIVE DIRECTORS
Uwe Marquardt, Christoph Barth

ART DIRECTOR
Hans-Jürgen Kammerer

COPYWRITER
Robert Junker

PHOTOGRAPHER
Elisabeth Herrmann

ADVERTISING SUPERVISOR
Jürgen Krautwald

LOCATION
Frankfurt, Germany

A great campaign for Amnesty International to drive home the horror that in too many places in the world people are locked up in appalling conditions simply because their religious beliefs, skin colour or opinions differ from those of the regime under which they live. The campaign consisted of pairs of model hands gripping the grille of street drains – as though a person were imprisoned beneath.

Our aim was to draw attention to human rights violations. These life-like hands were attached to drains at the traffic lights of Frankfurt's most frequented crossroads. Due to this activity, 860 people signed up on Amnesty International's subscription lists to protest against all countries that arrest or torture people because of their faith, opinion or skin colour.

JÜRGEN KRAUTWALD, AMNESTY INTERNATIONAL

TITLE
Goals

CLIENT
Nike

AGENCY
KesselsKramer

LOCATION
Amsterdam, The Netherlands

Chalk 'goals' appeared on brick walls in Amsterdam during the spring of 1996, accompanied not by copy but by the familiar Nike 'swoosh'. Strategy director Matthijs de Jongh of Dutch agency KesselsKramer explains the logic of the campaign: 'By drawing goals with chalk Nike wanted to inspire kids in the suburbs of Amsterdam to create their own football pitch with minimal resources. With this initiative Nike promoted the "Just do it" spirit in a simple way. This idea was executed in 1996 when it was still uncommon to think in media other than posters, print ads or commercials.'

TITLE
Skyline

CLIENT
Air Tahiti Nui

AGENCY
Saatchi & Saatchi,
New York

To advertise flights from NYC to
Tahiti, Saatchi & Saatchi commissioned
illustrator Dennis Clouse to create single-
line drawings depicting images that were
unmistakably of New York (in this case the
Manhattan skyline) and that fused into
something typically Tahitian. Here, the
illustration has been manufactured in
metal and mounted on a brick wall.

CREATIVE DIRECTORS
Tony Granger,
Sarah Barclay

ART DIRECTORS
Robert Perillo,
Danielle Thorton

COPYWRITER
Rob Lenois

ILLUSTRATOR
Dennis Clouse

LOCATION
New York, USA

TITLE
For the City

CLIENT
Cell C

AGENCY
Net#work BBDO

Many agencies and brands around the world have used graffiti methods such as stencilling to bring their campaigns on to the street in an engaging way. Few, however, have invested in the culture of street art as impressively as this campaign from BBDO's Johannesburg outpost. 35 huge artworks – essentially giant banners – by local 'street' artists were erected on the sides of buildings in downtown Johannesburg in 2003 to promote the mobile phone network Cell C. Entitled 'For The City', the project demonstrated the idea that the network was not merely rooted in the culture of the locality, but that it also recognized and supported it. The artworks are all still in place.

This campaign was so successful that Net#work set up a new branch in Johannesburg called New#tork in order to produce work with a specifically African flavour, drawing on local street culture of arts and crafts previously unharnessed by advertising.

CREATIVE DIRECTOR
Mike Schalit

ART DIRECTOR
Jonathan Santana

COPYWRITER
James Cloete

LOCATION
Johannesburg,
South Africa

Junction Box   1971

steel, paint, wiring, electricity.
100 x 120 x 50cm

www.britart.com

Pavement   1962

concrete slabs, cement, shoe prints,
dog excrement, chewing gum.
8000 x 15050 x 10cm

Regimented mosaic.
Companion piece to road by the same artist.

art you can buy **britart.com**

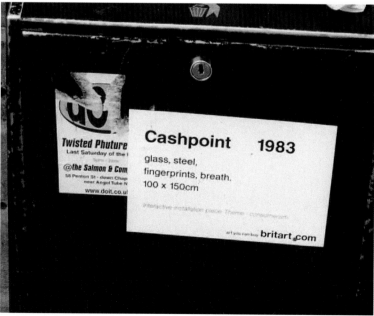

Cashpoint   1983

glass, steel,
fingerprints, breath.
100 x 150cm

interactive installation piece. Theme - consumerism.

art you can buy **britart.com**

Lamp Post

steel pole (hollow), glass,
dog urine.
200 x 10 x 10cm

art you can buy

TITLE
Britart

CLIENT
Britart.com

AGENCY
Mother

LOCATION
London, UK

This campaign dates from 2000. To encourage traffic to the website britart.com, agency Mother stuck up hundreds of labels around London, targeting the everyday objects that make up the fabric of urban life. Each label identified the object in question in artspeak, as if it were an exhibit in a gallery. Thus a tree became an 'Organic sculpture generating oxygen. A metaphor for life itself,' while a cashpoint was labelled 'Interactive installation piece; theme: consumerism.' The ads recall the joke in which a security guard's chair is mistaken for an exhibit, while also reminding us that art is indeed all around us. Mother also produced 'artalizers', or stickers to turn whatever you want into art – from 'CD Player' to 'Badly Dressed Person' – and also art pencils, the message being that you can make anything art, simply by writing or drawing on it.

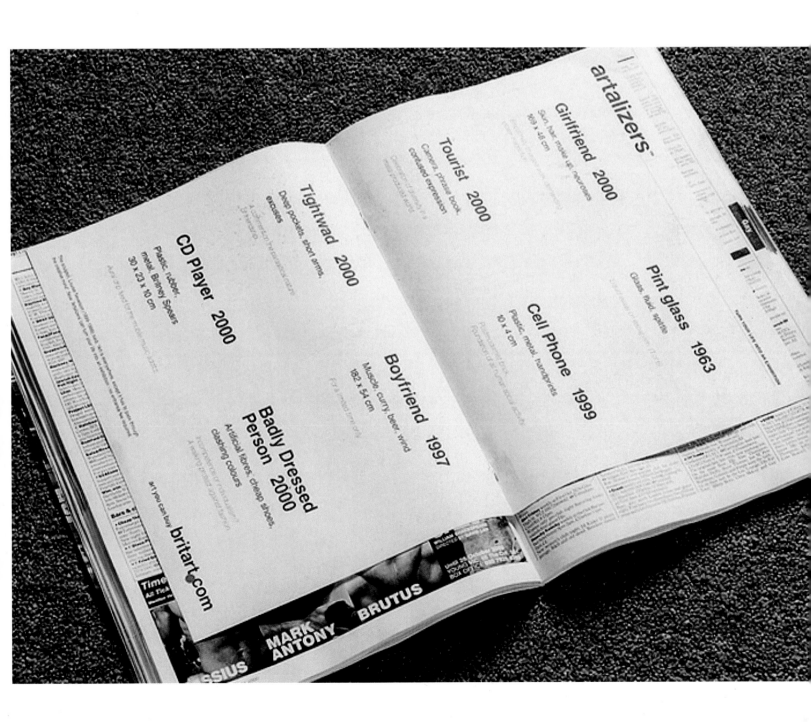

TITLE
Nike iD Reuters Sign

CLIENT
Nike iD

AGENCY
R/GA

PROGRAMMING
QA Ephraim Cohen,
John Mayo-Smith,
Sean Lyons, Scott Prindle,
Chuck Genco, Michael
Shagalov, Todd Kovner

INTERACTION DESIGN
Aya Karpinska,
Richard Ting

VISUAL DESIGN
Brian Votaw, Laura Pence,
Troy Kooper, Matthew
Garton, David Alcorn,
Johanna Rustia

COPYWRITERS
Mike Spiegel, Josh
Bletterman, Scott Tufts

ANALYTICS
Briggs Davidson

PRODUCTION
Andy Bhatt,
Matt Howell

LOCATION
New York, USA

As part of its promotion for the relaunch of nikeid.com – the site that enables consumers to custom-design trainers – agency R/GA created this interactive experience, mounted on the huge 23-storey digital billboard on the Reuters building in Times Square. Passers by were able to call a special number that was featured on the sign, and then use their mobile phone as a virtual mouse to create a design for the Nike Free 5.0 trainer, using a modified palette of colours. As participants pressed buttons on their phones, so the colours on the on-screen image of the shoe changed in real time. Once a design was completed, the user's phone received a text message that included a link whereby they could download mobile wallpaper of their freshly designed shoe, complete with a Times Square message to serve as a souvenir of the experience (this was after all 'the world's first cellphone-controlled, commerce-enabled interactive experience', as the agency put it). The text message also contained a unique PIN code and a text link that served as a gateway page into nikeid.com. By entering the code on this page, users were able to retrieve their Times Square creation with the option to further customize the shoe, and then actually to buy it. On the last day of the campaign Nike hosted a 'Friday Free For All', when they gave away Nike Free 5.0 trainers to every caller over a four-hour period.

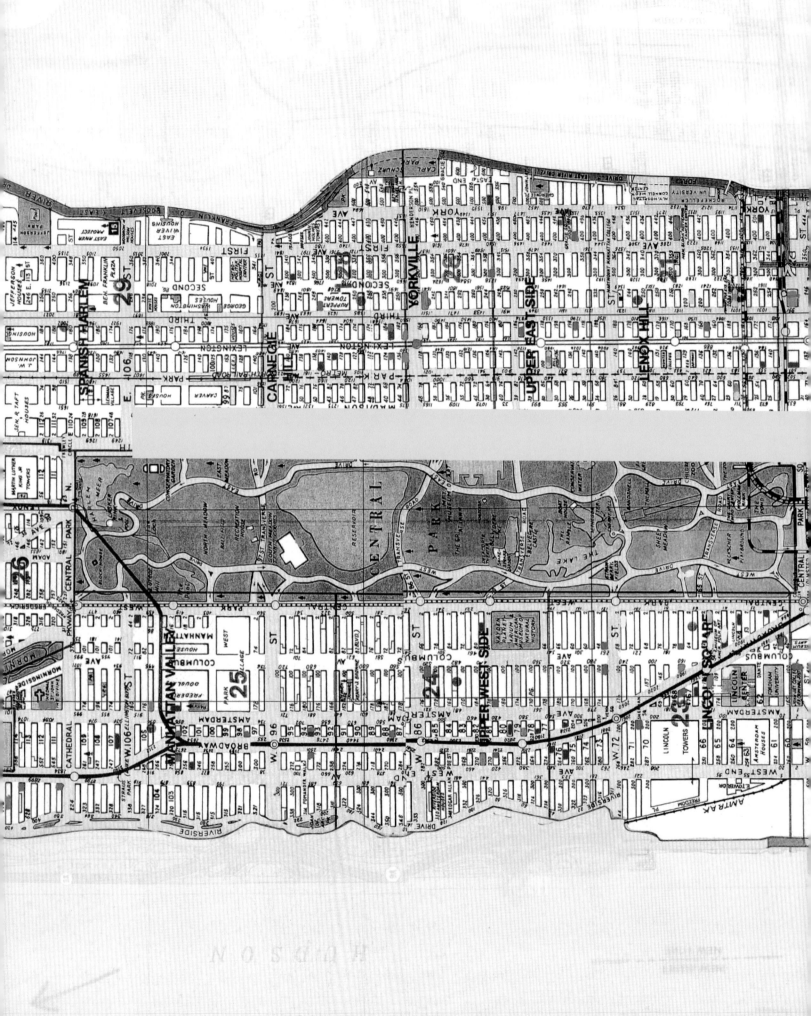

SITE-SPECIFIC MEDIA

To support the Nike TV campaign for Nikespeed.com, You're Faster than youThink, Publicis Mojo in Melbourne, Australia, commissioned two local street artists to create graphics showing characters needing to get somewhere fast. Artists Adam Cruickshank (Regular Product) and Cailan both produced two characters, each with an obvious ailment that requires them to reach a soothing destination – fast. These character stickers were then placed near an appropriate location, such as a bin (Vomit), an area of water (Bees), a toilet (Curry Man) or a drinking fountain (Chilli). The stickers all incorporate a long arrow, with the words 'You're Faster than youThink' running along the length of it, pointing directly to the desired destination.

TITLE
You're Faster
than youThink
CLIENT
Nikespeed.com
AGENCY
Publicis Mojo

ART DIRECTOR
Selena McKenzie

CREATIVE DIRECTOR
Darren Spiller

COPYWRITER
Toby Moore

ILLUSTRATORS
Adam Cruickshank,
Cailan Burns

ACCOUNT HANDLER
Kellie Lennon

BRAND MANAGER
Ed Elworthy

LOCATION
Melbourne, Australia

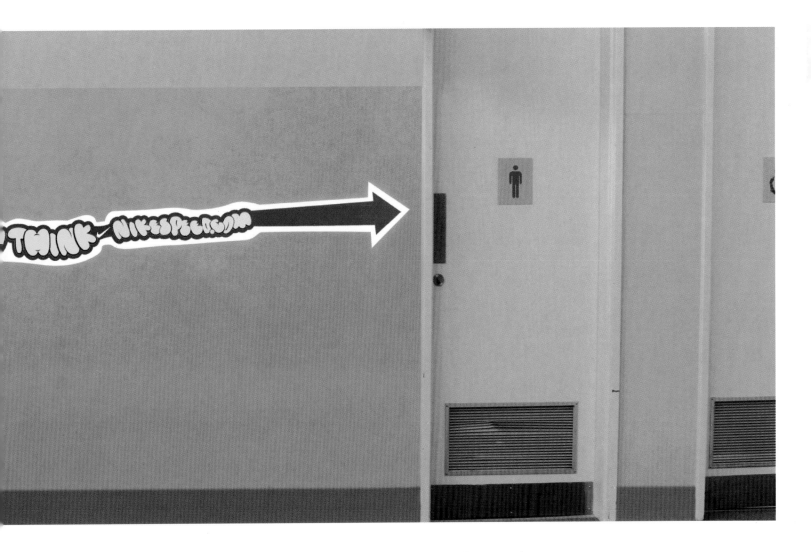

PLEASE DON'T SPEED NEAR SC

TITLE
Windscreen Flyer

CLIENT
Environment Waikato

AGENCY
Colenso BBDO

CREATIVES
Toby Talbot, Leo Premutico

PHOTOGRAPHER
Julian Wolkenstein

ILLUSTRATOR/TYPOGRAPHER
Ben Lockwood

LOCATION
Waikato, New Zealand

In this seriously hard-hitting campaign, over-sized flyers were placed, image-side down, on the windscreens of cars parked near schools in the Waikato region of New Zealand. Drivers returning to their cars would see only the white back of the flyer until they climbed inside – at which point they were confronted with the sight of a windscreen shattered by the impact of a horrifically injured child, accompanied by the simple, polite request, 'Please don't speed near schools.'

'Urban speeding is a real problem in small town New Zealand,' explains Toby Talbot, 'and some of the biggest culprits, ironically, are parents who rush to drop their kids at school each morning.' Simply reducing speed really does save lives, and the combination of extremely emotive imagery – of a driver's and a parent's worst nightmare – and the calm copy gets this message across succinctly and chillingly.

TITLE
Drink Driving Ends Here

CLIENT
Pedestrian Council of Australia

AGENCY
Saatchi & Saatchi, Sydney

Australia's roads are becoming
increasingly safe – the reason, according
to road safety researchers, being mainly
due to the good response to drink-driving
campaigns such as this one from Saatchi &
Saatchi. Black skid marks lead from the
road, up onto pavements and straight into
bus shelters, park benches or brick walls –
and the words 'Drink driving ends here.'

CREATIVE DIRECTOR
David Nobay

ART DIRECTOR
Jay Benjamin, Andy DiLallo

COPYWRITERS
Jay Benjamin, Andy DiLallo

LOCATION
Australia

TITLE
Parallel Bars/Rings

CLIENT
Adidas Singapore

AGENCY
FCB Singapore

CREATIVE DIRECTORS
Rob Sherlock, Robert Gaxiola

ART DIRECTOR
Dali Meskam

COPYWRITER
Hari Ramanathan

PHOTOGRAPHER
Cedric Lim

LOCATION
Singapore

Just as a puppy isn't just for Christmas, Adidas's Forever Sport campaign was designed to let consumers know that sport is ever-present – no matter where they are or what the occasion. Hence these sporting references in the least sporty of environments. The dangling rings for standing passengers to steady themselves on a commuter train make immediate reference to gymnastic rings simply by slapping the brand's logo and the campaign's strapline next to them. Similarly, metal railings make reference to parallel bars with the aid of an adjacent campaign sticker.

TITLE
Submerged
Hoarding/Loo

CLIENT
Fame Adlabs

AGENCY
Contract

CREATIVE DIRECTOR
Raj Nair

ART DIRECTOR
Shruthi Gopalakrishnan

COPYWRITER
Sriram Athray

PHOTOGRAPHER
Raj Mistry

LOCATION
Mumbai, India

These two ads are the fruit of Indian ad agency Contract's determination to find new ways and new places to advertise for their client Fame Adlabs, a huge five-screen multiplex cinema in Mumbai.

For the Indian cinema release of the global disaster movie *The Day After Tomorrow*, they placed a billboard in the sea, just off the beach, with the title and release date visible above the waterline. A buoy nearby in the background happens to look like the top of a submerged skyscraper, adding to the effect. 'The spire in the background is neither photoshopped nor did we put it there,' explains creative director Ashutosh Karkhanis. 'It has always been there. It's a post to which fishermen tie their boats.'

To promote the release of *Spiderman 2* in India, meanwhile, male cinema-goers were confronted with a urinal that only Spidey himself could possibly reach: amusing and impossible to ignore. Copywriter Sriram Athray witnessed some reactions to the installation: 'One guy actually asked the toilet attendant if the urinal was functional.'

CREATIVE DIRECTORS
Ashutosh Karkhanis,
Niranjan Kaushik, Raj Nair

ART DIRECTOR
Ashutosh Karkhanis

COPYWRITER
Niranjan Kaushik

PHOTOGRAPHER
Ashutosh Karkhanis

ACCOUNT HANDLERS
Vikas Bahl, Amrita Daru

LOCATION
Mumbai, India

The client had almost no money – but necessity is the mother of invention. In the end it cost less than £500 to print and distribute 20,000 cards.

TOM SPICER, CREATIVE, M&C SAATCHI

TITLE
Cab Cards

CLIENT
cabnumbers.com

AGENCY
M&C Saatchi

CREATIVES
Sergio Martin,
Tom Spicer

TYPOGRAPHY
Simon Warden

LOCATION
London, UK

Authentic-looking taxi business cards, which on closer inspection were for fictional firms such as Risk-A-Rape Taxis, were left in phone boxes, restaurants and bars as part of a campaign for licensed taxi service finder cabnumbers.com. Each card drew on frightening statistics such as the fact that 18 women are raped or sexually assaulted in illegal taxis every month in London. The cards featured a number to text so that the numbers of three local licensed cab operators could be returned to the user, thus making travelling in cabs a safer option.

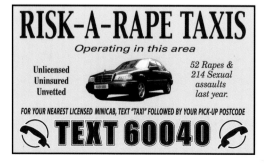

TITLE
Smart — Surprisingly
Spacious

CLIENT
DaimlerChrysler
Vertriebsorganisation
Deutschland

AGENCY
Springer & Jacoby Werbung

CREATIVE DIRECTORS
Bettina Olf, Tim Weber

ART DIRECTOR
Simone Eiteljörge

COPYWRITER
David Leinweber

PHOTOGRAPHERS
Jonas von der Hude,
Anja Heineking,
Maik Beimdiek

LOCATION
Germany

Three different sun screens were designed to be left in the windscreens of parked Smart cars, each using clever photography to create the impression of looking into the interior of a far larger vehicle – in this case a limousine, in the other two a caravan and even a bus. A stylish and witty use of screens designed to shade the interior of cars on hot days.

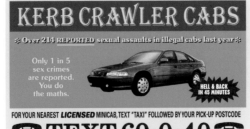

TITLE
Save the Children
Lorry

CLIENT
Save the Children

AGENCY
M&C Saatchi

ART DIRECTOR
Jim Hilson

COPYWRITER
Toby Allen

PHOTOGRAPHER
Nick Veasey
www.nickveasy.com

LOCATION
UK

In this clever use of lenticular technology by M&C Saatchi from 2003, the poster, covering both sides of the lorry, initially shows piles of wooden crates which the casual observer assumes to be the truck's contents. As the vehicle moves, however, the lenticular reveals another image: an X-ray of the crates, showing the huddled figures of small children who have stowed away inside them. Stencilled text on the back of the lorry tells us: 'Every year millions of children are trafficked for forced labour or sexual exploitation'.

In this case the medium is the message. People are trafficked illegally in lorries so this was the natural place to highlight the problem. X-ray images and lenticular technology combine to produce an eye-catching and thought-provoking message.

JIM HILSON, ART DIRECTOR, M&C SAATCHI

TITLE
Floats/Leaves

CLIENT
Olympus Australia

AGENCY
Saatchi & Saatchi,
Sydney

CREATIVE DIRECTOR
Malcolm Poynton

ART DIRECTOR
Matt Hazell

COPYWRITER
Jane Atkinson

PRODUCER
Trish Burgo

ACCOUNT HANDLER
Paul Mendham

MARKETING MANAGER
Bill Andreas

LOCATION
Australia

Normally small objects, such as leaves and swimming pool armbands, were literally made ten times bigger to demonstrate the 10X optical zoom power offered by a new Olympus camera. These oversized models were then left strategically in public locations where they could hardly be missed – together with a small sign with the message about the zoom power of the Olympus C-740 Ultrazoom camera.

TITLE
Money
CLIENT
Trimline Security Glass
AGENCY
Rethink

CREATIVE DIRECTORS
Ian Grais, Chris Staples
ART DIRECTOR
Rob Sweetman
COPYWRITER
Bryan Collins
PRODUCER
Pat Busswood
LOCATION
Vancouver, Canada

To promote the security glass produced by a local company, Canadian agency Rethink ingeniously treated a bus shelter's Adshel with a shatter-resistant coating, and filled it – apparently – with banknotes to the value of over three million Canadian dollars. In fact most of the bills were fake, with about $500 in real bills making up the top layer.

'The reaction was extraordinary,' recalls copywriter Bryan Collins. 'Almost everyone who walked by ended up kicking, punching and body-checking the glass. People returned hours later with their families. The following morning we hit the front page of the *Vancouver Sun*. Then the news stations started showing up in earnest. We made the 5:00 news on every station and nationally on several networks. Since then, the story has run in countless newspapers and magazines around the world. All this for a $6,000 CDN investment.'

TITLE
Light Bulb

CLIENT
The Economist

AGENCY
Abbott Mead Vickers
BBDO

This special-build poster, which appeared in London late in 2004, featured a giant, three-dimensional light bulb against *The Economist* magazine's trademark red background – alluding, of course, to the bright brains of those who read it. The bulb lit up every time someone passed directly beneath it, as Paul Belford explains: 'It actually works on the same principle as security lights. There's a small sensor hidden by the bulb that detects movement [which is] triggered whenever a pedestrian walks beneath it.'

CREATIVES
Paul Belford,
Nigel Roberts

LOCATION
London, UK

TITLE
Evian Lido

CLIENT
Evian

AGENCY
Cake

CREATIVE DIRECTOR
Mark Whelan

LOCATION
London, UK

When Brockwell Lido was set to close permanently in 2001, Cake client Evian stepped in to sponsor it, matching owner Lambeth Council's £100,000 investment that year to improve it and keep it open – and of course make it a huge branding opportunity. The logo was clearly visible from the various flight paths above London, and Cake organized a variety of events, ranging from Evian-sponsored kids' lifeguard lessons to a big party with Basement Jaxx headlining.

TITLE
Nike Speed
CLIENT
Nike
AGENCY
Ogilvy

Anyone walking past this row of six Adshels taken over by Nike in Singapore might have wondered what exactly the sports brand was advertising. A strange pattern forms a stripe across each poster, which is otherwise white apart from a small Nike logo in the top right-hand corner. This intriguing pattern invites investigation. Only when you see the final Adshel on the far right of the series, and notice the front of a trainer looking as though it's bursting through the actual structure of it, does it become clear that the set of posters is designed to give the impression that a Nike trainer has ripped through all of them like a speeding bullet.

CREATIVE DIRECTOR
Craig Smith
ART DIRECTORS
Naoki Ga, PeiPei Ng
LOCATION
Singapore

TITLE
Nature Calls Map

CLIENT
Nike

AGENCY
Wieden + Kennedy

CREATIVE DIRECTORS
Ty Montague,
Todd Waterbury

ART DIRECTOR
Kim Schoen

COPYWRITER
Ilicia Winokur

LOCATION
New York, USA

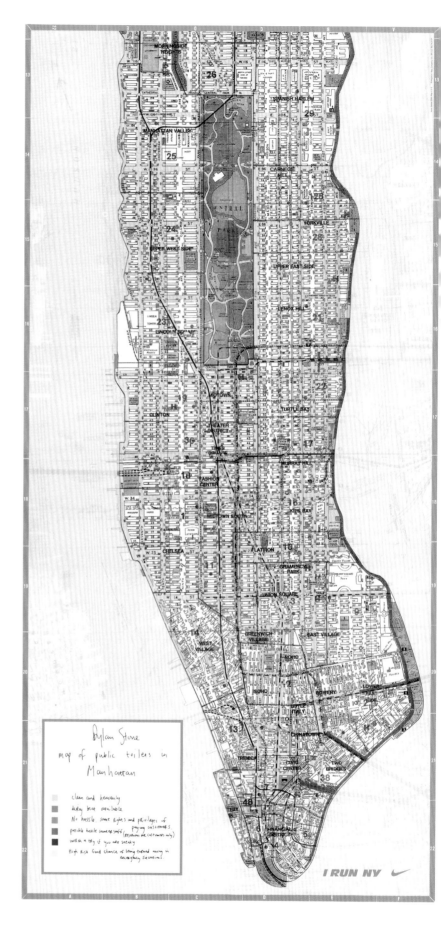

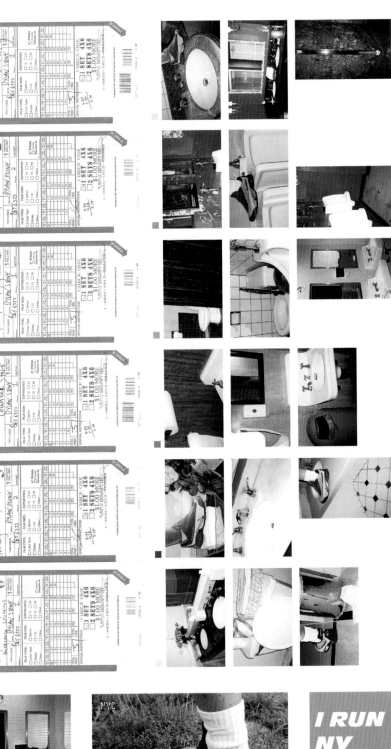

These maps were created as a functional gift to runners in the New York Marathon in 2003. All urban runners will know the importance of having a good place to use as a pit stop, so the maps helpfully point out a selection of places where runners can stop and relieve themselves. To collect this information, creatives from W+K went out and scoured the city for runner-friendly rest rooms, rating them according to runner-relevant criteria and even photographed them. The end result may look confusing to the untrained eye – but not, we're assured, to runners.

MYC

I RUN NY

THE NATURE CALLS MAP. BECAUSE EVERY NOW AND THEN YOU HAVE TO GO TO THE BATHROOM DURING A RUN.

THE AIR DRI GOAT BY NIKE IS BUILT TO WITHSTAND NATURE'S WORST ELEMENTS AND THE BUMPS, POTHOLES AND UNEXPECTED DETOURS OF A NEW YORK CITY RUN.

TITLE
Graffiti

CLIENT
Procter & Gamble – Ariel

AGENCY
Saatchi & Saatchi, London

EXECUTIVE CREATIVE DIRECTOR
Tony Granger

CREATIVE DIRECTOR
Sarah Barclay

ART DIRECTORS
Linda Choi, Kerstin Grahl

COPYWRITERS
Jaime Schwarz, Sue Ann Ho

PHOTOGRAPHY
Alex Coley

ACCOUNT MANAGER
Rebecca Minns

ACCOUNT DIRECTOR
Vicky Graham

TRAFFIC MANAGER
Ben McMullen

LOCATION
London, UK

Graffiti artist Moose has been much in demand from advertising agencies over the past couple of years. This is because rather than using paint to give form to his stencil shapes, he uses detergent to clean away the grime of the city and reveal clean shapes on dirty walls or pavements.

'This campaign was all done in one afternoon and these images were all taken around Abbey Road and Belsize Road in North London,' reveals Moose. ' It took much longer than one afternoon to find suitable locations though – ie two points from which to "hang" the clothes line – two trees, two lamp posts that were situated against a surface that would respond to my cleaning methods.'

The beauty of this campaign is that cleaning walls isn't illegal or defacing. It was only a matter of time before a bright spark at an agency thought to actually apply this idea to a cleaning product. Here we see washing lines and noticeably clean clothes strung up on dirty walls and fences. Good, appropriate use of media/medium and adventurous stuff for Procter & Gamble.

TITLE
Snow Plough/
TripleThick

CLIENT
McDonald's

AGENCY
Leo Burnett,
Chicago

CREATIVE DIRECTOR
John Montgomery

ART DIRECTOR
Brian Shembeda

COPYWRITER
Avery Gross

PRODUCTION ON
SNOW PLOUGH
Denis Giroux,
Laurie Gustafson

PRODUCTION ON TRIPLE THICK
Laurie Gustafson

PHOTOGRAPHER
Greg Mohrs

LOCATION
Chicago, USA

To launch McDonald's Arctic Orange Triple Thick milkshakes in Chicago, Leo Burnett came up with two local campaigns to underline the coldness and also the thickness of the shake. In the sweltering heat of August 2004 they rolled out the city's famous orange snow ploughs, emblematic of the bitter cold of winter in Chicago, to advertise the shake. Then, in the Triple Thick campaign, they cleverly used a billboard to boast about the thickness of the drink. The post that supports the billboard was adorned with a stripe that perfectly matched the straw in the image, so enhancing the illusion of an upside-down drinks carton containing a drink so thick that it doesn't simply fall out.

TITLE
Ballerina

CLIENT
Joffrey Ballet School

AGENCY
Saatchi & Saatchi,
New York

This idea is so simple that it hardly needs explanation. New York's Saatchi & Saatchi office came up with this clever use of a revolving door as the animation tool that makes a life-size image of a ballerina actually dance: when the door revolves, the ballerina pirouettes. Why? To promote the city's Joffrey Ballet School, of course.

CREATIVE DIRECTORS
Tony Granger,
Barbara Boyle

ART DIRECTORS
Menno Kluin,
Paul Kwong

COPYWRITERS
Jens Paul Pfau,
Glen Levy

PHOTOGRAPHER
Dedjora Jutz

LOCATION
New York, USA

TITLE
Really, Really Big Cake
CLIENT
Kraft Foods
AGENCY
JWT São Paulo

More ingenious use of unconventional media space – a great idea from JWT São Paulo's office for Kraft Food's Royal baking powder: taking over two huge walls of this bizarre-shaped building and making it look as if it's a cross-section of a massive cake. This campaign instantly turned the building into a landmark and a talking point, while staying brilliantly relevant to the product.

CREATIVE DIRECTOR
Átila Francucci

ART DIRECTOR
Luiz Risi

COPYWRITER
Vítor Patalano

PHOTOGRAPHY
Dulla

ART BUYER
Cecília Quirico

GRAPHIC PRODUCERS
Jomar Farias and
Fábio Sato

ACCOUNT SERVICE
Fernanda Antonelli,
Fernanda Tedde,
Thais Leon

LOCATION
São Paulo, Brazil

FURNISHED BY IKEA.

EW YORK.

TITLE
Absolut New York

CLIENT
Absolut Vodka

AGENCY
TWBA\Chiat\Day

CREATIVE DIRECTOR
David Page

ART DIRECTORS AND COPYWRITERS
Jackie End,
Bill Montgomery

CREATED BY
Atomic Props

INSTALLATION BY
Artkraft Strauss

LOCATION
New York, USA

This incredible 5.8 x 15-metre (19 x 49-foot) billboard appeared on the corner of Lafayette and Bond Street in New York in the summer of 2000, and stayed there for the rest of the year. The billboard showed a life-size studio flat in the shape of an Absolut vodka bottle, filled with furniture supplied by IKEA, complete with living room, bathroom, kitchen, a working TV and computer, magazines on the coffee table and even leftover Chinese take-away food cartons. '[It's] a pretty good-size apartment,' observed Richard Lewis, then worldwide account director on the brand for TBWA\Chiat\Day, New York. 'Actually it's a great place to live, but the rent is a bit steep – $12,000 a month.'

At around the time of this ad, Absolut was a leading player in unconventional or ambient advertising. There was a 4.3-metre (14-foot) Absolut bottle on Sunset Boulevard, and another on a suburban highway in Miami, the latter being part of an ongoing performance piece involving painting the bottle with a thousand layers of paint, with adjacent letters spelling out the word Absolut. In Chile in 1999, TBWA planted a field of flowers in the shape of the now iconic bottle, dubbing the piece Absolut Summer. Since then, the UK has seen executions for the brand such as Absolut Zero, a bottle-shaped ice rink, and Absolut Chilled, a bottle-shaped igloo built of ice outside a shopping centre in Manchester, into which shoppers could go to try freezing vodka served in glasses made of ice.

SNEAKY MANOE UV-RES

SNEAKY MANOEUVRES

ART DIRECTORS
Johan Landin,
Andreas Ullenius

COPYWRITER
Mark Ardelius

ACCOUNT DIRECTORS
Kjell Månsson,
Andreas Engstrand

ACCOUNT MANAGER
Marie Höglin

LOCATION
Stockholm, Sweden

TITLE
Pram
CLIENT
UNICEF Sweden
AGENCY
åkestam.holst

Not all infants are registered at birth, particularly in remote villages. And if officially they don't exist, then they may be easy victims of child abuse. To promote a campaign by UNICEF to raise awareness of this issue, agency åkestam.holst left a number of empty prams in the streets of Stockholm. As people passed by they triggered the sound of a baby crying. When they leaned over to look at the baby, they found instead the disquieting information that 'Every day 136,986 children are born who do not exist', accompanied by a voiceover calling for support for the child registration campaign.

Though it created a powerful metaphor for non-existent children, this campaign lasted only three days before confused police started to collect up the prams. This was not before a major newspaper had given it coverage. UNICEF collected some 2,000 new 'World Parents' who give monetary support on a regular basis in the immediate aftermath of the campaign.

TITLE
Grocery Divider

CLIENT
Gold's Gym

AGENCY
Rethink

In this entertaining local campaign by agency Rethink for a branch of Gold's Gym near Vancouver, the grocery dividers in a supermarket round the corner from the gym were lead-weighted to make them far heavier than usual, and branded with the name of the gym. The result was that most shoppers struggled to pick them up and move them – so highlighting the potential to tone up those biceps.

'The idea here is simply to try and take the gym's message out of the gym,' explains copywriter Bryan Collins. 'There are two ways to interpret the message from this grocery divider. It could be as simple as "Lift weights – Gold's Gym". But what we really wanted was for people to have that moment where they can't lift something they really should be able to, and think: "Man, I need to get to the gym". It's a funny prank that gets people thinking about their fitness and uses a medium in a way nobody is expecting.'

CREATIVE DIRECTORS
Ian Grais, Chris Staples

ART DIRECTOR
Rob Sweetman

COPYWRITER
Bryan Collins

PRODUCTION
Natalie Freer

LOCATION
Vancouver, Canada

TITLE
Smelling Billboard

CLIENT
Affinity Petcare –
Advance Dog Food

AGENCY
Michael Conrad
& Leo Burnett

CREATIVE DIRECTOR
Manfred Wappenschmidt

ART DIRECTOR
Daniela Skwrna

COPYWRITER
Hasso Von Kietzell

LOCATION
Frankfurt, Germany

Rather than succumb to the cliché
of producing a TV spot for dog food
showing a floppy and oh-so-glossy
Labrador leaping blithely around a sunny
park (in slow motion), Michael Conrad &
Leo Burnett in Frankfurt produced these
dog-height posters that were treated to
smell absolutely delicious – if you were a
dog, that is. Thus it was that dogs, tails
wagging, led their owners to the ads,
before demonstrating that they could
still do that puppy-dog eye thing. Which
of course is the doggy equivalent of
emotional blackmail…Can't think of
a better ad for dog food.

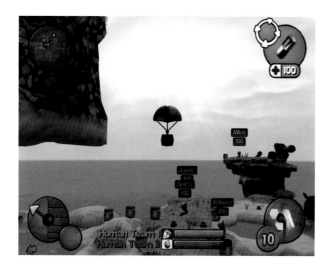

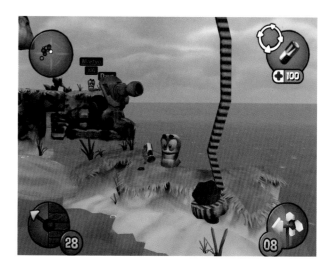

Experiential and very definitely unconventional, these two campaigns demonstrate that the gaming environment is an interesting developing media space for brands.

Launched at the end of 2003 on PS2, Xbox, Gamecube and PC, Worms 3D contained a unique, at the time, piece of branded content. Players control teams of heavily armed Worms, ensuring they blow the stuffing out of each other using a huge variety of weapons. Throughout the game, supply crates parachute into the landscape, each containing a potentially useful weapon, tool or health pack. This is where Red Bull comes in. The energy drink in its iconic blue and silver can appears in the game as one of the available 'power-ups'. When a player selects a can of Red Bull, their health value is boosted by up to 100 per cent and they become much faster in both attack and escape modes.

So here we see Red Bull being drunk and providing health and performance benefits – exactly the kind of claims that the brand has not been allowed to make in its TV campaigns.

TITLE
Worms 3D/Judge Dredd: Dredd vs Death
CLIENT
Red Bull
AGENCY
Hive Partners

SITUATION PLACEMENT CONCEPT
AND IMPLEMENTATION
Ed Bartlett

The Worms 3D Red Bull project was the first-ever example of what we call 'situation placement', so called because we work together with the game developer on behalf of the advertiser to create a bespoke scenario or 'situation' within the fabric of the gameplay or game storyline itself, where the product (in this case energy drink Red Bull) can be seamlessly integrated. The critical elements ... are contextual relevance and providing some kind of gameplay benefit to the end user for interacting with the product. In the case of Worms 3D the title was specifically chosen by matching both consumer demographic and gameplay characteristics with that of the Red Bull product.

ED BARTLETT, HIVE PARTNERS

Launched about the same time as Worms 3D in late 2003, Judge Dredd: Dredd vs Death sees the inclusion of Red Bull in the gaming environment in a different way. The game is played through Dredd's eyes as he patrols the mean streets of the futuristic metropolis MegaCity One, dealing with litterers, loiterers, junkies and worse, while also looking to save the city from the evil Judge Death. In order to keep the populace in check, stimulants, such as caffeine, are controlled substances.

Step in Red Bull. The drink is being smuggled illegally, according to Judge Dredd's harsh ban on stimulants, into the city and the player needs to keep control of suppliers handling the product in the city's docklands. Gangs of Red Bull 'dealers' are notably more agile, better shots and altogether harder to subdue than other characters in the game. Red Bull logos appear on crates, and glowing graffiti logos are 'tagged' on walls where 'dealers' want to attract custom.

We are again dealing with branded content here, but 'product benefit' takes a more indirect form than in Worms 3D.

If you look at any big US movie
there'll be brands all over it.
In this film you won't be able to
tell Meltin' Pot are involved really.
It's about a story and an idea.

RANKIN, CREATIVE DIRECTOR, MELTIN' POT

A successful film can be the most
powerful vehicle for conveying even
the most complex messages...[it] gives
us both the opportunity to support a
great cinema project and to be highly
innovative in terms of conveying the
Meltin' Pot brand to an eclectic audience.

AUGUSTO ROMANO, COMPANY DIRECTOR, MELTIN' POT

This project sees Italian jeans brand Meltin' Pot hook up with photographer, publisher and now director Rankin to create a feature-length film. Ostensibly an exercise in branded content, the film features clothes from the brand's Spring/Summer '06 collection. But this film, on paper at least (at the time of writing it was still in post production), doesn't offer the usual kind of brand content. *The Lives of the Saints* is a real film, with a good script and a plot that leans towards magical realism, offering an engaging alternative to the catwalk parade favoured by most fashion brands.

The strategy for Meltin' Pot's communications for the season, from billboards to TV commercials, is set to revolve around the movie and its principal characters, whose wardrobes feature items from the season's collection. So while posters and trailers for the film will promote a promising piece of cinema, viewers will be exposed to the brand's new collection. The season's look books were all shot by Rankin on the film set.

So how did this project come about? Company director Augusto Romano originally approached Rankin, the brand's creative director, to make a short film. Rankin's response was to embark on an extensive search for a full-length script (aided by a script competition held through *Dazed and Confused* magazine), eventually settling on one written by Tony Grisoni, author of the screenplay for Terry Gilliam's *Fear and Loathing in Las Vegas*.

TITLE
The Lives of the Saints

CLIENT
Meltin' Pot Jeans

AGENCY
Dazed Film &TV

DIRECTORS
Rankin and Chris Cottam

PRODUCER
Laura Hastings-Smith

WRITER
Tony Grisoni

EXECUTIVE PRODUCER
Augusto Romano

DIRECTOR OF PHOTOGRAPHY
Baz Irvine

FILM EDITOR
Chris Gill

PRODUCTION DESIGNER
Mark Digby

COMPOSER
Rob Lane

SOUND DESIGN
Paul Davies

CASTING DIRECTOR
Rosalie Clayton

LEADING PLAYERS
James Cosmo, David Leon, Emma Pierson, Bronson Webb, Sam MacLintock, Daon Broni, Gillian Kearney and Marc Warren.

Seattle's new hover
Don't fight traffic, figh

VIA EXPRESS

3443

s!

gravity!

TITLE
Science Fiction
Launch Campaign

CLIENT
Seattle Science Fiction
Museum and Hall
of Fame

AGENCY
Cole & Weber / Red Cell

Seattle's Science Fiction Museum and Hall of Fame was opened in 2004 to pay homage to the genre, with displays ranging from Captain James T. Kirk's command chair to costumes from *Planet of the Apes*. To publicize the museum, Cole & Weber/Red Cell decided to do exactly what the genre tends to do: blur the lines between fact and fiction. The ads they created teased Seattle with campaigns promoting futuristic products and services, but set in contemporary Seattle landscapes. Postcards promoting Seattle Transit's new 'Hover Bus' displayed a photo of a Seattle street complete with a futuristic hovering bus, while poster ads showing a rocket ship ready for take off against the backdrop of the Seattle skyline boasted the headline: 'Elliott Bay Lunar Vacations. Leave your troubles 240,000 miles behind!'

The campaign also featured posters placed in empty store fronts to advertise the business that was supposedly about to open on the premises, complete with logos and lists of services available. Eye-catching new retail outlets included 'Intergalactic Alien Pet Imports', Seattle's largest supplier of 12-eyed sycophish, shipped daily from Epsilon Prime.

CREATIVE DIRECTOR
Guy Seese

ASST. CREATIVE DIRECTORS
Jim Elliott,
Todd Derksen

ART DIRECTORS
Todd Derksen,
Travis Britton

DESIGN
Dylan Bernd,
Craig Erickson

COPYWRITER
Jim Elliott

PRINT/PRODUCTION
Peter Calandra,
Kristi Lyons,
Gregory Radcliffe

RADIO/PRODUCTION
Nicole Hartshorn

RADIO/AUDIO
Eric Johnson (Clatter
& Din – Seattle)

PHOTOGRAPHY
David Clugston

ILLUSTRATION
Stephan Martiniere
(Rhythm & Hues, LA),
Sean Onart

DIGITAL ART
Sean Onart

ACCOUNT MANAGEMENT
Dave Behn, M.J. Keehn

LOCATION
Seattle, USA

This had huge stopping power on the streets as people were trying to figure out if it was for real or not.

BRAD HARRINGTON, COLE & WEBER/RED CELL

STUN-
TS

102-157

 情熱を制す者が、ゲームを制す。

TITLE
Vertical Football

CLIENT
Adidas

AGENCY
TBWA\Japan

Two footballers, suspended high above the Tokyo streets, play a death-defying game as they attempt to score goals past each other, kicking a football, also suspended on a rope, against the backdrop of a huge green billboard. This was a stunt that proved impossible to ignore: traffic came to a standstill as people stopped to check out the action and take photographs. The stunt received coverage on local and international news channels.

CREATIVE DIRECTOR/ COPYWRITER
John Merrifield

ART DIRECTORS
Clementine Tourres,
Hirofumi Nakajima

PRODUCTION MANAGER
Akinori Otani

LOCATION
Tokyo and Osaka, Japan

TITLE
It's Raining Men

CLIENT
Cleo magazine

AGENCY
Maverick

CREATIVES
Simon Kirkham,
Grant Hunter

LOCATION
Melbourne and Sydney,
Australia

Australian women's magazine *Cleo* briefed agency Maverick to encourage their readership to vote in their Bachelor of the Year promotion in April 2002. Maverick came up with this campaign, It's Raining Men. And that's exactly what happened. A whopping 10,000 near-naked Ken dolls (as in Barbie) were attached to carefully filled helium balloons (so that they descended gently) and dropped over the beaches and shopping areas of Melbourne and Sydney.

The dolls were dressed only in white boxer shorts, and each bore a tag linking him with a radio promotion and also with one of the bachelors featured in *Cleo*. Bemused and amused women caught the dolls to check them out – but did this campaign work? Readership of the magazine increased 12 per cent over the previous issue, while there was an 8 per cent response to the voting numbers attached to the dolls. And of course the sight of several thousand Ken dolls floating to the ground in two major cities was picked up by local news networks.

TITLE
The World's First
Inflatable Church

CLIENT
The Protestant
Church

AGENCY
Jung von Matt
Stuttgart

You're camping out under the stars
And there's nothing but you and the sod –
No street names, no shops and no cars,
It's a place to feel closer to God.
For religion's more precious than gold;
It's the only true end of your search.
So blow and behold
A glory untold,
The world's first inflatable church!
Yes, religion's more precious than gold
And the only true end of your search.
You just blow and behold
A glory untold,
The world's first inflatable church!

Or perhaps you're sat out at the back
And it looks a good day for the barbie.
Till the sky starts to loom very black;
It's as nasty as Robert Mugabe;
But with God as your chargé d'affaires
You will never be left in the lurch.
Let it rise like a prayer
On the beckoning air,
The world's first inflatable church!
Yes with God as your chargé d'affaires
You will never be left in the lurch.
It will rise like a prayer
On the beckoning air,
The world's first inflatable church!

JOHN WHITWORTH

Get more people into Church is a brief that most creatives would baulk at. Not so, however, at agency Jung von Matt. Creatives Joachim Silber and Paul Fleig decided that if the people weren't going to church, they'd bring the church to the people. Literally. Thus, the first ever fully portable and inflatable church was created. It has appeared on golf courses, airports, in car parks and all manner of locations, turning more heads than a streaker at the vicar's tea party. Not only has it inspired poetry, you can even hire it for your wedding.

Visit www.inflatablechurch.com to find out how.

CREATIVE DIRECTORS
Achim Jäger, Peter Waibel

ART DIRECTOR
Joachim Silber

COPYWRITER
Paul Fleig

DESIGNER
Andreas Jeutter

PHOTOGRAPHER
Marcus Stadler

LOCATION
Germany

TITLE
Homesick?

CLIENT
Emirates

AGENCY
Saatchi & Saatchi,
Sydney

In this amusing campaign for Emirates
airlines, designed to target sunbathing
Brits, a stunt plane was employed to fly
over the sea off Sydney's Bondi Beach,
leaving a vapour trail that looked like rain
falling from a cloud. A billboard truck
then paraded up and down the beach
bearing the message: 'Homesick?
We fly to the UK 77 times a week'.

CREATIVE DIRECTOR
David Nobay

ART DIRECTOR
Steve Carlin

COPYWRITER
Scot Waterhouse

LOCATION
Sydney, Australia

TITLE
Red Carpet

CLIENT
Sitges Sci-Fi & Fantasy
Film Festival

AGENCY
Leo Burnett, Madrid

CREATIVE DIRECTORS
Javi Alverez, Fernando Martín

ART DIRECTOR
Miguel de María

COPYWRITER
Francisco Cassis

LOCATION
Sitges, Spain

To celebrate B-movie star Godzilla's 50th anniversary, Sitges Sci-Fi & Fantasy Film
Festival decided to mark the occasion with this bizarre, but intriguing, campaign by
Leo Burnett, Madrid. The aim was to draw attention to the Godzilla-themed events
taking place during the festival. A red carpet ran through the seaside town of Sitges,
emerging from the sea to lead up the beach, on to the roads and directly to the festival's
main venue. The idea, of course, was that Godzilla, who always emerges from the sea,
would be given the red carpet treatment should he deign to make an appearance.
Signs suspended high up in trees warned Godzilla to leave them alone, while another
above a high bridge counselled the VIP monster to mind his head.

To advertise the television show *CSI: Crime Scene Investigation*, Saatchi & Saatchi set up fictitious crime scenes in high-traffic areas such as public rest rooms, parking lots, public beaches and train stations. The scenes were all cordoned off with bright yellow police-style tape, which on closer inspection revealed details of the show. My favourite is the blood-soaked suitcase sticking out of a locker.

DO NOT CROSS

CSI 9PM WED AXN

DO NOT CROSS

CSI 9PM WED AXN

In this campaign for British Airways, M&C Saatchi
brought various London landmarks to European cities.
In Paris, passers by who stopped to look at the work of an
artist who seemed to be drawing the Eiffel Tower would
discover images of the Houses of Parliament and Big Ben
on his sketch pad, while the back of his director's-style
chair bore the words: 'London is closer than you think'.
In one Paris Metro station a poster was devised to create
the illusion that a hole in the wall led to a London tube
station beyond. Meanwhile, red pillar boxes emblazoned
with the Swedish equivalent of the campaign's strapline,
'Ingen har fler avgångar till London', ('Nobody has more
departures to London') appeared in Stockholm, and a
poster in Copenhagen bearing the campaign slogan had
sensors which were triggered by passers by and called
out to them in unmistakably London voices. A Metro
station in Milan was dressed to look like a London
Underground station, while above ground in the city,
black cabs drove around bearing the words 'Londra è
più vicina di quanto pensi'. Double-takes guaranteed…

TITLE
London is Closer
than you Think

CLIENT
British Airways

AGENCY
M&C Saatchi

ART DIRECTOR
Shane Gibson

COPYWRITER
Simon Dicketts

PHOTOGRAPHER
Alan Mahon

LOCATIONS
Barcelona, Berlin, Cologne,
Copenhagen, Dusseldorf,
Milan, Paris, Rome and
Stockholm.

Unlike in the UK, where BA is something of a sacred cow, in Europe it is a challenger brand, snapping at the heels of Alitalia, Air France and so forth. This allowed us to be much more provocative and intrusive than is usual for the airline. The comparatively small budget also insisted that the work got noticed. The publicity this campaign received was sensational.

SIMON DICKETTS, COPYWRITER, M&C SAATCHI

TITLE
Departure Lounge
CLIENT
United Airlines
AGENCY
Fallon London

CREATIVE DIRECTORS
Andy McLeod,
Richard Flintham
CREATIVE
Ali Alvarez
ILLUSTRATOR
Erik Sandberg
LOCATION
London, UK

Fallon turned a section of London's Bank Underground station into a departure lounge to promote United Airlines: as people walked past a check-in desk, about to enter a corridor of tunnel, they were handed leaflets and brochures by uniformed air stewards who welcomed them 'on board'. Fallon commissioned illustrator Erik Sandberg to create over 150 painted views as if seen from an aeroplane window, which were placed along the adjacent tunnel to add to the aeronautical illusion.

This was an opportunity to break up the tedium of people's daily commute…The space lent itself to the idea and then we just made it as interesting, engaging and playful as possible.

ALI ALVAREZ, CREATIVE, FALLON LONDON

TITLE
Toy Box

CLIENT
BMW Asia Pacific

AGENCY
TBWA\Singapore

Ah, the Mini: it's famously
small and fun, so here it
is packaged like a big toy
to appeal to that part of
potential customers that
has never grown up.

CREATIVE DIRECTORS
Robert Kleman,
Marcus Rebeschini

ART DIRECTOR
Marcus Rebeschini

COPYWRITER
Robert Kleman

ACCOUNT SERVICE
Robin Nayak

LOCATION
Singapore

TITLE
Taxi Launderette

CLIENT
Unilever Home and
Personal Care –
Robijn

AGENCY
PPGH/JWT

With great original
thinking, agency PPGH/
JWT in Amsterdam
converted the hubcaps
on several taxis to look
like washing machines:
real clothes, real water,
real detergent, real suds,
great use of media.

CREATIVE DIRECTORS
Peter Clercx, Stephan
Propper, Lion Versloot

CREATIVES
Daan Booister, Marc van
Wageningen, Jasper Jager

ACCOUNT
Michiel van de Graaff, Kiek
Berger, Hellen de Lange

ACCOUNT PLANNING
Quirine Faber

PRODUCTION
Fast Media

LOCATION
Amsterdam, The
Netherlands

TITLE
Ice Polo

CLIENT
Volkswagen

AGENCY
DDB London

A life-size model of the Volkswagen Polo Twist made entirely of ice was 'parked' outside the Saatchi Gallery on Belvedere Road in London in May 2004. The stunt by VW's agency DDB was to promote a free air-conditioning offer over the summer, and images of the ice car were used in a four-week national press advertisement.

Carved from nine and a half tonnes of ice imported from Canada, the sculpture took three sculptors around 350 hours to create, working in temperatures of minus 10 degrees Celsius (14 degrees Fahrenheit) in a huge freezer. Once installed on Belvedere Road the ice car, all eight and a half tonnes of it, took just 12 hours to disappear.

Philip Hughes, managing director of Ice Box (the company who created the sculpture) commented: 'We have worked on hundreds of projects for major brands throughout the UK and Europe, mainly for live communications and events. However, the Polo Twist is the largest project for a specific shoot and single piece of advertising.'

CREATIVE DIRECTOR
Jeremy Craigen

ART DIRECTORS
Graeme Hall,
Gavin Siakimotu

COPYWRITERS
Gavin Siakimotu,
Graeme Hall

PHOTOGRAPHER
Graeme Hall

LOCATION
London, UK

TITLE
Eggs
CLIENT
Virgin Atlantic
AGENCY
Net#work BBDO

This stunt by Virgin Atlantic aimed to get the message over to flyers that their luggage handling isn't perhaps as brutal as that of their competitors. Whether you could actually put two dozen eggs in the hold on one of their flights and still expect to be on good terms with fellow passengers after the baggage reclaim experience seems somewhat dubious… But that's precisely the point: Virgin Atlantic demonstrate they can wittily talk the talk and provide comic relief towards the end of the flying experience, in a place guaranteed to be the focus of all passengers' attention.

This was a truly guerrilla tactic whereby these trays were placed on the carousels of rival airlines to score a competitive point about Virgin's superior service. None of the eggs were hard-boiled. NET#WORK BBDO

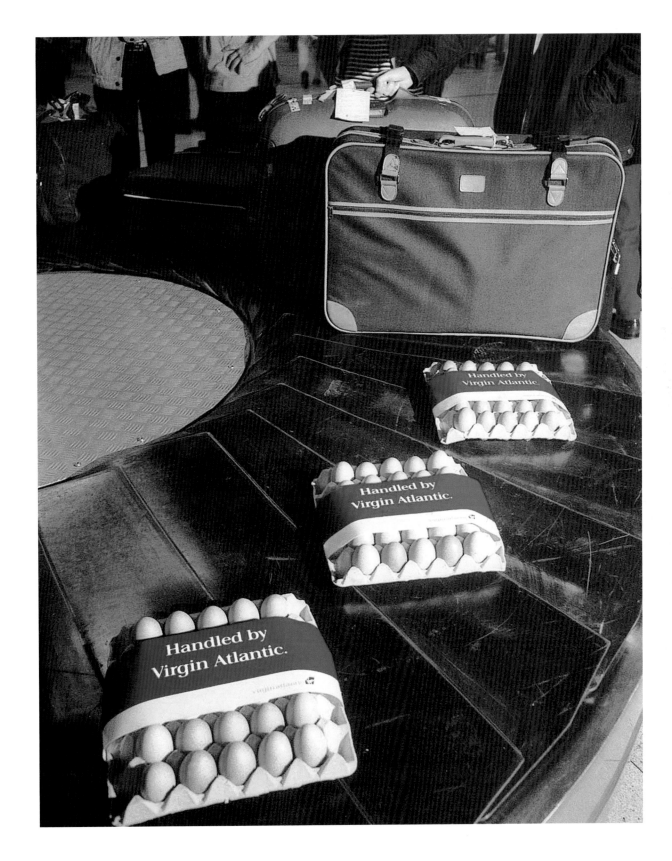

CREATIVE DIRECTOR
Mike Schalit

ART DIRECTOR
Theo Ferreira

COPYWRITER
Alistair Morgan

LOCATION
Johannesburg,
South Africa

TITLE
Radar Van

CLIENT
FBI Recruitment

AGENCY
Saatchi & Saatchi,
Sydney

Saatchi & Saatchi made the most of
their client's name in this campaign.
White vans bearing the advertising
recruitment firm FBI's name – complete
with radar-style dishes on their roofs –
were parked outside the Sydney offices
of the big networks. The idea being that
FBI Recruitment know what's going on
inside ad agencies and are therefore
perfectly placed to recruit for them – so
specifically targeting them in a way that
advertising folk would acknowledge.

CREATIVE DIRECTOR
David Nobay

ART DIRECTORS
Jay Benjamin,
Andy DiLallo

COPYWRITER
Charlie Ross

LOCATION
Sydney, Australia

A pick-up truck zooms past on the highway, pursued by what appear to be three heat-seeking missiles. Not a scene from a James Bond movie, but a campaign for action movie specialist TV channel CH-9 by JWT Malaysia. The missiles are actually helium-filled balloons attached by cords to the truck, which as they fly behind it create the illusion of three missiles in hot pursuit. This took Grand Prix in the Outdoor category at the Cannes International Advertising Festival in 2004.

TITLE
Missile Car
CLIENT
CH-9 Media
AGENCY
JWT Malaysia

CREATIVE DIRECTORS
Edwin Leong,
Andy Soong
ART DIRECTORS
Andy Soong, Raymond Goh,
Edwin Leong
COPYWRITERS
Hasnah Mohd. Samidin,
Wong Sen Kiat, Joel Lim
PRODUCTION MANAGER
Hin Kee Yong
PHOTOGRAPHER
Looi Wing Fai
LOCATION
Malaysia

TITLE
Driverless Delivery Van
CLIENT
Simba Ghost Pops
AGENCY
Net#work BBDO

This caused quite a few double-takes. Inspired by the name of this kids' snack, the windows of the cab of the white delivery truck were doctored so that it appeared driverless as it drove around making deliveries.

CREATIVE DIRECTORS
Julian Watt, Mike Schalit

ART DIRECTOR
Marion Bryan

COPYWRITER
Asheen Naidu

PHOTOGRAPHERS
Gerard Turnley, Michael Meyersfeld

TYPOGRAPHER
Marion Bryan

LOCATION
Johannesburg, South Africa

TITLE
Impossible Bus Pull

CLIENT
Adidas

AGENCY
TBWA\Japan

CREATIVE DIRECTOR
John Merrifield

ART DIRECTORS
Tadashi Tsujimoto,
Hirofumi Nakajima

COPYWRITER
Katsuhisa Fujita

FACILITATOR
Akinori Otani

ACCOUNT SERVICE
Steven Horowitz, Taro Sato

CLIENT
Soichi Shirakawa, Adidas

LOCATION
Tokyo, Osaka, Nagoya,
Fukuoka and Sapporo, Japan

To raise awareness of the unconventional campaign idea Impossible is Nothing for Adidas, TBWA\Japan produced the Impossible Bus Pull, a precursor to Vertical Football and Impossible Sprint (pages 104–5 and 154–5), featuring buses customized to include the line that is now synonymous with Adidas. Rather than describe the spirit of Impossible is Nothing, this stunt demonstrated it: strongmen pulled the buses, though members of the public were invited to have a go too. Not surprisingly, it attracted a fair bit of publicity in the process.

Buses would be driven in the wee hours of the morning to the day's destination (outside stadiums on game days, in high pedestrian traffic locations, etc.) and then be pulled from 8am throughout the day.

JOHN MERRIFIELD, CREATIVE DIRECTOR, TBWA\JAPAN

KesselsKramer launched this still topical campaign back in 2001. The idea is simple: 'Make Trade Fair' and other slogans relevant to the idea of promoting fair trade were stencilled on huge metal shipping containers – which, of course, symbolize global trade and are highly visible at ports, harbours and other busy trade centres.

TITLE
Make Trade Fair

CLIENT
Oxfam

AGENCY
KesselsKramer

LOCATION
Global

TITLE
Singing Tower
CLIENT
J-Wave Radio
AGENCY
Dentsu

J-Wave is a Japanese radio station based in the imposing Tokyo skyscraper, the Roppongi Hills Mori tower. Agency Dentsu came up with the idea of creating a fully functional graphic equalizer display using 300 green lights placed high up in windows over several upper floors of the building, visible for miles around. In early October 2003, intrigued locals spotting the pulsating lights turned on their radios to find that the display was synchronized perfectly to J-Wave's live audio output. The display became a talking point in the city as photos and messages were sent between friends on mobile phones and posted on Internet blog sites.

This is so freaking amazing, the only thing I'm thinking about is just to stare at it for the rest of my life! Dooooood!

CREATIVE DIRECTORS
Takuya Isojima,
Masayoshi Kubo

ART DIRECTOR
Masayoshi Kubo

COPYWRITERS
Takuya Isojima,
Yutaka Tsujino

DESIGNERS
Kanako Moriyama,
Yoko Sasaki

PRODUCTION COMPANY
J.C. Spark

LOCATION
Tokyo, Japan

TITLE
The Ass of Commons

CLIENT
FHM magazine

AGENCY
Bartle Bogle Hegarty

ART DIRECTOR
Adam Scholes

COPYWRITER
Hugh Todd

**PRODUCTION
COMPANY**
Cunning Stunts

LOCATION
London, UK

This is one of the most memorable guerrilla campaigns of recent years to take place in London. A naked woman projected on to the Houses of Parliament makes a perfect recipe for media coverage and that all important 'talked about' factor. But what was the campaign for? Men's magazine FHM publishes a readers' poll of their 100 Sexiest Women each year: this stunt was to raise awareness of the poll in 1999. The woman projected, TV presenter Gail Porter, got a very respectable top ten rating, reaching number eight.

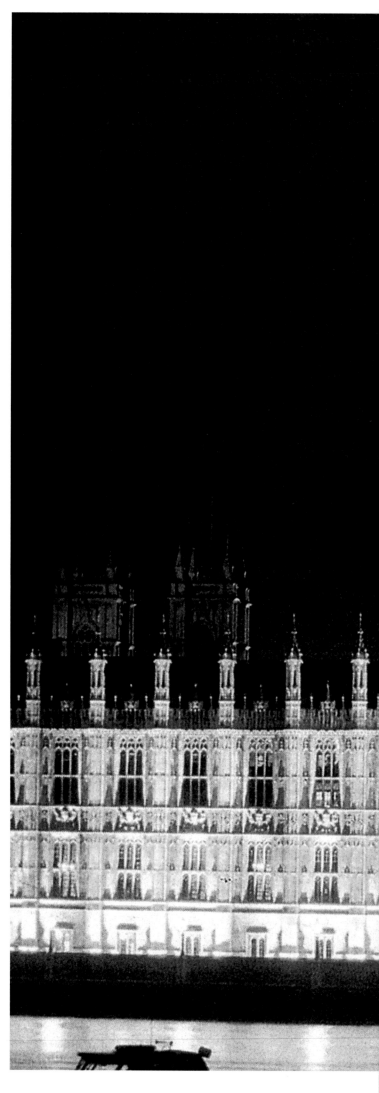

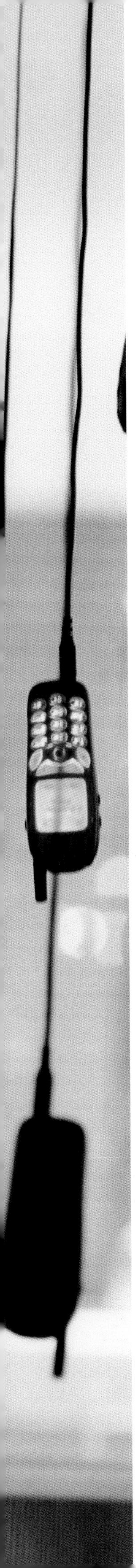

TITLE
Digital Aquarium
CLIENT
Motorola
AGENCY
The Fish Can
Sing/Digit

The Fish Can Sing called upon new media
and interactive specialists Digit to create
the Digital Aquarium to help promote
the aesthetics of Motorola's v70 model.
An interactive exhibit made up of 150
suspended handsets, the Digital
Aquarium stood outside London's Design
Museum for eight weeks in 2002. When
passers by called one of several special
numbers (printed on the outside of the
tank in which the installation was
housed), phones lit up and vibrated in
sequence, resembling a shoal of fish.

DESIGN AND BUILD
Digit
LOCATION
London, UK

This street campaign from Dutch agency StrawberryFrog was designed to demonstrate how people can maximize their space at a minimal price if they shop at IKEA and embrace IKEA's 'Go Cubic' concept. 18 living room installations appeared overnight in 12 different Dutch cities with IKEA shops. Each installation was set in 8.5 square metres (91 square feet); the size of an average parking space, and included a resident eating breakfast, reading the paper and chatting to passers by. And if that wasn't enough to cause a stir, the 'residents' at each of the installations encouraged passers by to 'steal' the furniture and take it home with them.

TITLE
Go Cubic

CLIENT
IKEA

AGENCY
StrawberryFrog

CREATIVE DIRECTOR
Mark Chalmers

ART DIRECTOR
Hadleigh Averill

PRODUCER
Carl Panczak

PHOTOGRAPHER
Paul Barbera

LOCATION
The Netherlands

IKEA's seasonal push was all about maximizing space for a minimal price so their catalogue featured living spaces of different sizes appropriately fitted out.

We took this idea beyond the catalogue and kitted out car parking spaces in high streets throughout Europe – one of the few spaces recognized globally – a pure 8.5 m sq. kitted out in quirky IKEA furniture. We generated more press, foot traffic and drive-by viewing in three days than a three-month street poster campaign. The client was blown away.

MARK CHALMERS, CREATIVE DIRECTOR, STRAWBERRY FROG

TITLE
Be Proud of your Loo

CLIENT
Reckitt Benckiser – Harpic

AGENCY
JWT London

CREATIVE DIRECTORS
Nick Bell, Charity Charity

WRITER
Laurence Quinn

ART DIRECTORS
Mark Norcutt, Adam Griffin

ACCOUNT HANDLER
Sam Southey

PLANNER
Olivia Heywood

LOCATION
London, UK

JWT created the line 'Be proud of your loo' and placed this spoof ad in an estate agent's window – the idea being that the vendor is so proud of their toilet that they consider it the number one selling point of their property. Seeing a photo of just a toilet on property details in the window of an estate agency is bound to intrigue even the least curious of people. On closer inspection, the accompanying info read thus:

'Knightsbridge, SW1. Large bathroom with Rimjet toilet. Extraordinary performance from a 3-inch flush valve. Silver fittings, anti-slam toilet seat & dual flush option. Price £350 pw. Tel: 0207 935 7712. Harpic. Be proud of your loo.'

Continuing the theme, JWT also ran a classified ad using similar text in the 'Flats to let' section of the *Evening Standard* newspaper: advertising in forms and places that you'd least expect.

TITLE
Move It

CLIENT
Which?

AGENCY
Hicklin Slade & Partners

In April 2004, *Which?*, the magazine of the British Consumers' Association, and agency Hicklin Slade & Partners set up Cheatem & Ripoff, a blatantly rogue estate agency designed to demonstrate to the public the lack of regulation governing the activities of British estate agents. BBC TV and radio, Channel Five, Sky News and national newspapers including the *Daily Mail*, *Daily Express*, *Guardian*, *The Times* and *Financial Times* covered the stunt, and online coverage included BBC online and Guardian Unlimited. Essentially it threw down the gauntlet to the government, demanding a crackdown on unscrupulous practices. *Which?* Director of Campaigns and Communications, Nick Stace explains: 'It's madness. I've had no training in the property market and I've no knowledge of the Estate Agents Act. But I can set up and sell homes. Dodgy practice has left the public exposed to the unchecked, often illegal whims of rogue estate agents for far too long.'

Following the campaign, the British government undertook to cut the proposed two-year wait before a full investigation into the state of the industry was carried out.

CREATIVE DIRECTORS
Adam Haywood,
Malcolm Caldwell

ART DIRECTOR
Adam Haywood

COPYWRITER
Malcolm Caldwell

PLANNING
Mark Runacus

ACCOUNT DIRECTORS
Andy Hunt Cooke,
Mark Khoo

PRODUCTION
Iain Clarke,
Janna Perryman

LOCATION
London, UK

TITLE
Impossible Sprint

CLIENT
Adidas

AGENCY
TBWA\Japan

The follow-up to the Vertical Football stunt in Tokyo in 2003 (see pages 104–5), Impossible Sprint saw 100-metre sprint tracks appear on the sides of Hong Kong and Shanghai skyscrapers. Competitors winched their way up ropes, one per lane, to reach the top of the track as fast as possible, the winner of the final bagging $10,000. The stunt was picked up and reported on by news programmes around the world.

CREATIVE DIRECTOR
John Merrifield

ART DIRECTORS
Shintaro Hashimoto,
Hirofumi Nakajima,
John Merrifield

LOCATION
Hong Kong and
Shanghai, China

Working hours in Hong Kong are long, with many people working a 55-hour week. This means that most professionals get less than the recommended eight hours of sleep, which in turn leads to trouble in getting out of bed in the morning. This campaign from agency DDB's Hong Kong office featured a young office worker slumbering peacefully in a bed placed in a busy metro station. Beside the sleeping woman was a picture of a McDonald's breakfast meal, with the copy: 'Having trouble getting going in the morning? Start your day right with a McDonald's breakfast.'

'Breakfast is the meal that really defines how much energy you'll have to start your day off right,' explains the agency, 'but, incredibly, our target demographic tends to skip it, or grab a very light meal on the go. The task of this advertising was to shatter complacency and get people to "wake up" to the value of a great breakfast.'

The campaign won a Gold Award for innovative idea of the year in the MTR (Hong Kong metro) Awards, was featured in the magazine *Advertising Age* as an international idea of the month, and received extensive coverage in the Hong Kong press.

TITLE
Bed

CLIENT
McDonald's

AGENCY
DDB Hong Kong

CREATIVE DIRECTORS
CC Tang, Steven Lee, Derek Wong

COPYWRITER
Derek Wong

ART DIRECTOR
Edmond Chan

DIRECTOR OF OPERATIONS
Peter Rodenbeck

LOCATION
Hong Kong, China

MULTI
FRON
ED
ATTAC

MULTI-FRONTED ATTACK

158–187

TITLE
Beta-7

CLIENT
SEGA/ESPN

AGENCY
Wieden + Kennedy
New York

Beta-7 was a remarkable campaign created to launch Sega's American football game 'ESPN NFL Football'. Targeting hardcore video gamers, it comprised a number of live and interactive elements that played out online and in real time over a four-month period.

The premise was that a games tester, who called himself Beta-7, had been testing a new first-person American football game but had found himself having bizarre physical reactions to it. He documented his experiences online at his own website, Beta-7.com, in which he suggested that the game was dangerous, and rallied support to halt its release. Soon after this two more sites appeared online, apparently set up by gamers who disputed Beta-7's site, and soon the gaming community was ablaze with discussion and much blogging on the subject. Was this games tester for real? Or was it some kind of marketing ploy?

Wieden + Kennedy worked with Haxan Films (producers of *The Blair Witch Project*) and Chelsea Pictures to cast actors to play the main roles in the campaign, including Beta-7 himself. The actors played their roles 24/7 for the entire four-month period of the campaign, answering posts on the blog, responding to emails and even being interviewed by the gaming press.

Meanwhile, as controversy over the Beta-7 site raged within the gaming community, Sega officials doggedly denied the very existence of the game. But as early as the testing stage, shredded documents from Sega officials, apparently found in Sega offices bins, were re-assembled, photographed and appeared online, so creating confusion and feeding both sides of the argument. Months before the campaign played out, the agency had even placed ads in local newspapers which were subsequently used to 'prove' that Beta-7 had responded to an ad to become a games tester for Sega.

The various sites continued blogging online, and the ongoing, long-term development of the campaign included viral videos, voicemails, posts at independent gaming sites, emails, TV commercials, small-space newspaper ads and flyers.

There is absolutely nothing conventional about this advertising campaign, which took the Grand Clio award in the inaugural Content & Contact category in 2004. Jury chairman Nick Brien, then CEO of Arc Worldwide Chicago, commented: 'The gaming community is highly cynical and media savvy: they don't want to be marketed to. The smart thinking behind the launch of the game was fantastically executed in terms of both contact strategy and very challenging content. The campaign really was an experience and the agency went out of their way to completely fuse content and contact thinking, and pulled it off brilliantly.'

W 63rd St. New
. My place of birth
. My date of birth
1942.

reby given that an
by the Civil Court,
nty, on the 4th day
01, bearing Index
CN2001, a copy of
examined at the
Clerk, located at 111
, in room 118, grants
to assume the name
DENNIS APONTE.
ame is Eduardo
te. My present ad-
Madison St. NY, NY
place of birth is NYC.
of birth is 11-22-88.

hereby given that an
red by the Civil Court,
County, on the 14 day
2003, bearing Index
784NCN03, a copy of
v be examined at the

available ___
& Tunnel Authority, 2 Broadway,
New York, NY 10004. Bids will be
taken until 3:00 PM on August 26,
2003. Interested parties should
contact Mrs Laura Jamison at
412-631-1063

NOTICE
If you or anyone you know has
volunteered in the last 2mos as a
Beta Tester for ESPN NFL
Football,call 415-507-7777 Your
response will remain confidential

PRAY TO ST. JUDE!
When all else fails, ask St. Jude to
pray for you and your prayers will
be answered!

LOST & FOUND
$100 Reward for White Gold and
Diamond ring. Lost at Abaya on
Houston and A or Korova Milk Bar

RESUME
CAREER COUNSEL

RESUMES
Create/Update/Sam
* * FREE JOB PLACEME
Call Deb 212-244-277

RESUME-WRITE $1
Fast makeover: reword &
High impact resume/lette
212-385-9369   139 Fult

**EMPLOYMEN
AGENCIES**

1 CASH CASH CA
Any one that needs cas
No Agency Fee. C
718-540-7660 212-5

AIRLINES NOW H
Flight Att-Tktng-Bag H
Paid train sal to $40

The smoking gun, baby.

Targeting hardcore video gamers, it comprised a number of live and interactive elements that played out online and in real time over a four-month period.

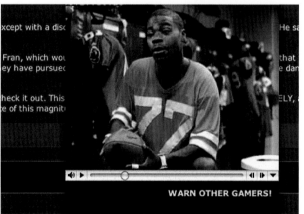

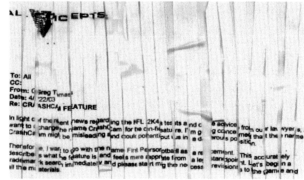

CREATIVE DIRECTORS
Ty Montague,
Todd Waterbury

ASSOCIATE CREATIVE
DIRECTORS
Kevin Proudfoot,
Paul Renner

ART DIRECTOR
Robert Rasmussen

COPYWRITER
Bobby Hershfield

ACCOUNT MANAGER
Erin Bradburn

EXECUTIVE PRODUCER
Gary Krieg

AGENCY PRODUCER
Temma Shoaf

AGENCY EDITOR
Andrew Robertson

PRODUCTION
ASSISTANT
Christopher Zei

PRODUCTION COMPANY
Chelsea Pictures,
Haxan Entertainment

EXECUTIVE PRODUCER
Steve Wax

PRODUCERS
Anthony Nelson of Chelsea
Pictures, Debra Kent and
Stephanie Bruni of MJZ

DIRECTORS
Mike Monello, Ed Sanchez

DIRECTOR OF PHOTOGRAPHY
Sal Totino

WRITERS
Mike Monello, Ed Sanchez,
Jim Gunshanon,
M.C. Johnson

EDITORS
Pete Beaudreau, Gavin
Cutler of Mackenzie Cutler

PRINCIPAL TALENT
Warren Sapp, Tracy Morgan

PHOTOGRAPHY/PROPS
Drew White

INTERNET CONSULTANT
GMS Studios by
Brian Clark

EDITING AND
POST EFFECTS
John Rice

NOW IT G

TS DISTURBING.

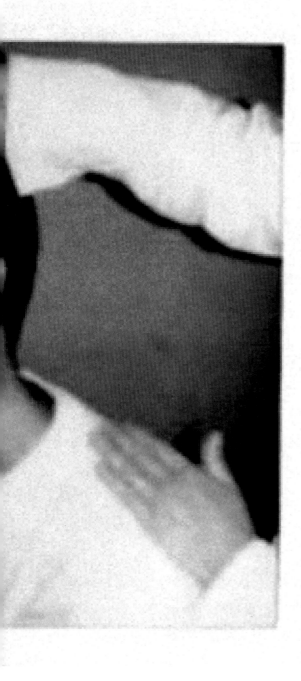

TITLE
HYPE

CLIENT
Hewlett Packard

AGENCY
Publicis

This campaign threw conventional approaches to advertising out of the window, and not just for the sake of doing something kooky. HYPE was a truly integrated marketing campaign, conjured up by Chris Aldhous and Peter Hodgson of Publicis in response to client Hewlett Packard's request for a campaign targeting young graphics professionals. But rather than producing a print or TV campaign, Aldhous and Hodgson kicked conventional approaches into touch and instead proposed creating an art gallery – 'a space where we could enable young people to show their work'.

Except that this gallery space would start off completely empty, apart from some large-format HP printers and projectors. Young designers, illustrators and film-makers would be encouraged to turn up at the gallery with their work, so that it could be hung or projected onto the blank walls. The result would be a constantly changing exhibition, at which exhibitors and spectators alike would witness not only a selection of imagery by different artists, but also the HP equipment facilitating it all.

'We wanted to position HP as the people who enable young creatives to get their work out,' comments Aldhous. HP would promise to credit and promote the work of young creatives through the exhibition and its marketing.

To kick off that marketing, Aldhous and Hodgson recruited Manchester graffiti artist Moose, who introduced the pair to clean graffiti. Using a stencil, he sprayed cleaning fluid onto dirty London walls and pavements so that the Hype logo, or parts of it, were reversed out of the city's grime. Moose also cut the logo into existing poster sites, stripping away layers of paper so that the word 'hype' appeared in the wood of the board behind. All this activity has the advantage of being legal, of course, as it doesn't involve adding layers of paint or sticking up posters.

A website was set up at www.hypegallery.com with details of the forthcoming free gallery space, encouraging young image-makers to produce a piece of A0 work to show there. Design blogs and notice boards were also targeted with images and information about the project.

Meanwhile, 20 emerging young image-makers were commissioned to produce works that would be based round the letters 'h' and 'p'. These were run in magazines with simply a credit for the image-maker and the web address. In partnership with ambient media specialists Diabolical Liberties, an ad hoc gallery was created on London's Old Street roundabout by mounting posters of some of these artworks on railings. In addition, information packs about the project were sent to art school tutors.

13 young filmmakers were also commissioned to produce short films in order to help kick-start film entries for the project. Six of these ran in London art house cinemas, while the others were screened on student TV channel JVTV. The films were also posted on the website, which in addition encouraged anyone interested in becoming involved in the show to post submissions online, which could then be projected or printed at the venue.

In yet another branch of the campaign, ads for some of the show's content – but made to look like typical Hollywood movie posters or art gallery ads – ran in *Time Out* magazine.

So did the campaign work? At precisely six o'clock on the evening of 22 January 2004, the doors of HYPE were thrown open to the public. 'That first evening about 120 artists turned up with their images,' recalls Aldhous. 'The first digital films also arrived and we uploaded them to the projectors in the Film Bunker.'

As art arrived at the gallery, a third phase of hypegallery.com went live. In this, the online community was able to wander round a virtual version of the gallery and check out the art that was being submitted. 'Over the next four weeks, HYPE spread around the world,' says Aldhous. 'The website had 4.5 million hits with 90,000 unique users from 142 different countries. 2,500 pieces of digital art were uploaded to the site. Back in Brick Lane, 1,193 artists submitted their work physically at the HYPE gallery. Of those, almost all of them returned to the venue at the close of the gallery to collect their prints, essentially HP print samples.'

HYPE Paris opened in the Palais de Tokyo in November 2004 and attracted 32,000 visitors. HYPE Moscow followed…

The experience will travel to cities all over the world, encouraging and promoting the work of young image- and filmmakers, while also offering a tangible demonstration of Hewlett Packard's products to that demographic, in a campaign that has become an aspirational piece of brand communication.

CREATIVES
Chris Aldhous,
Peter Hodgson

LOCATION
London, UK

20 emerging young image-makers
were commissioned to produce
works that would be based round
the letters 'h' and 'p'.

TITLE
Remember Rainier
CLIENT
Rainier Brewing Company
AGENCY
Cole & Weber/Red Cell

(TNT) MAX *Enemy at the Gates*
—Drama·*2:30* 951368 *p.M10*
(9) **That '70s Show**—Comedy 19287
Donna's short story makes Eric look bad.
(11) **Everybody Loves Raymond** 31455
Debra volunteers to help Marie cook a big
meal.

1:00 (11) **RainierVision**—Comedy 19985
Two Seattleites still in love with the beer their
dads grew up with find an old box of commer-
cials and take it to the people while discussing
all things Rainier.
(MSNBC) **MSNBC Investigates** *1:00* 98523
(CNB) **Suze Orman**—Discussion *1:00* 85504
(CNN) **CNN Presents** *1:00* 977184
Obesity in America.
(COM) **The Man Show**—Comedy 93813
A breast implant fashion show.
Mo Collins plays Lorraine, who ends up naked
and handcuffed at the beach; and Jewel in a
parody of her "Intuition" video.
(35) **Doctor Who**—Science Fiction 70815
"Terminus," Part 1 of four.
(39) **Grateful Dead: The Closing of Winter-**

(ES2) **NFL Live** 3741558
(FNC) **After Hours with Cal Tho**
(FX) **Hitchhiker Chronicles**—
(H&G) **Date with Design** 191720
A living room is recast.
(HAL) **Big Valley**—Western *1:00*
(HBO) MAX *Star Wars Episo*
the   Clones—Science
6925875 *p.M27*
(HB02) **Inside the NFL** *1:00* 4219
(HTS) **Modern Marvels** *1:00* 9119
Mars exploration technology is
(LIF) **What Should You Do?** *1:*
A woman survives being dragg
(MSN) **MSNBC Investigates** *1:*
(MTV) **True Life**—Documentary *1*
Young adults who rent beach h
(NIK) **Roseanne**—Comedy 8125
Christmastime brings Darlene
from Bev and D.J., and Beck
job.
(QVC) **Northern Nights**—Shopp
(SCI) MAX *Epoch*—Science Fict
3274233 *p.M10*

Rainier Beer was brewed in Seattle for some 180 years before the brand was bought out in the early 1990s. At this point the brewery at the gates of the city – a local landmark with its huge red neon 'R' on the roof – was closed, as production moved to California. The beer slowly disappeared from both store shelves and memories. Ten years later, following another change of ownership, the brand's new owners wanted to reintroduce it to the city of its birth, but had neither a big enough budget for new TV commercials nor any loyalty among young beer drinkers upon which to build.

Agency Cole & Weber/Red Cell's solution was to create a multi-faceted campaign based around an 11-episode late-night TV programme featuring two young Seattle guys, Tim and Chuck, who had supposedly discovered a box of old Rainier beer commercials in an attic, and

decided to champion Seattle's all-but-forgotten favourite beer of old. Rainier Vision (think *Wayne's World* with beer instead of electric guitars) aired late on Saturday night/Sunday morning, and involved them showing vintage TV commercials from Rainier's heyday while discussing all things Rainier and generally goofing around.

The TV show developed a cult following, partly as a result of the feedback mechanisms built into the programme: viewers could phone Tim and Chuck, leave voicemail messages or send emails via the RememberRainier.com campaign website. The site carries the faux vintage look and feel of the TV show, and provides endless entertainment and tongue-in-cheek Rainier trivia. It also directs viewers to the bars, stores and restaurants that gradually joined a burgeoning trend to restock Rainier beer across the city.

Tim and Chuck became local celebrities, and every weekend they were out promoting the show and talking with viewers and fans of their show in bars and at festivals and events. Three classic Rainier commercials were brushed down and aired on network and local television during sporting events and after game shows. A vintage-looking press kit was sent to local and national papers (one sold on eBay for $152), while a host of promotional materials, stickers, postcard flyers, T-shirts and key-chains helped the brand appeal to a 21–34-year-old demographic.

Perhaps the funniest part of the campaign was prompted by an incident in a national park campground, which hit the news worldwide in August 2004, when a black bear was discovered in a drunken stupor after downing a case of Rainier. Having found a stash of another beer and tried one, the bear decided to stick to Rainier and, 36 cans later, subsided into a peaceful slumber. Cole & Weber/Red Cell leaped on this unmissable PR opportunity, convincing the client to produce three genuinely hilarious low-budget TV commercials capitalizing on the event and featuring the actors from RainierVision.

CREATIVE DIRECTOR
Guy Seese

ASST CREATIVE DIRECTORS
Jim Elliott, Todd Derksen

ART DIRECTORS
Guy Seese, Todd Derksen,
Sunshine Stevens, Travis
Britton, Dylan Bernd

DESIGN
Dylan Bernd, Todd Derksen,
Nate Johnson, Jeremiah
Whitaker

COPYWRITERS
Guy Seese, Jim Elliott, Kevin
Thomson, Mike Tuton

PRODUCTION
Nicole Hartshorn,
Jessica Cohoon,
Kelly Showalter

TV/DIRECTION
Wyatt Neumann, Mike
Prevette, Jack Hodge,
Carol Hodge

TV/EDITING
Wyatt Neumann, Mike
Prevette, Matt Ralston

TV/PRODUCTION COMPANIES
Ellipsis Pictures,
Lenz Films, Alarming
Pictures (all Seattle)

TV/AUDIO
Eric Johnson
(Clatter & Din – Seattle)

TV/TALENT
Tim Hornor, Kevin Brady,
Mike Tuton

TV & WEB/MUSIC
Mick Philp (theme
song only)

PRINT & WEB/
DIGITAL ART
Sean Onart

WEB/DEVELOPMENT
Karl Norsen

ACCOUNT MANAGEMENT
Brenda Narciso, Jen Scott,
Megan Eulberg,
Megan Greene

LOCATION
Seattle, USA

TITLE
Subservient Chicken
CLIENT
Burger King
AGENCY
Crispin Porter + Bogusky

Visitors to www.subservientchicken.com, which launched in April 2004, are invited to 'Get chicken the way you like it', as the chicken, or rather man dressed as a chicken, stares expectantly at the camera. With a knowing nod to interactive webcam peepshow-style sites, the idea here is that you type in a command such as 'dance', and the chicken obeys you. Within limits. Not surprisingly, as this is after all a Burger King communication, there are things that the chicken won't do – and he lets you know by approaching the camera with an offended look, wagging a scolding finger.

Within the first 24 hours of going live, the site racked up a staggering million hits, which – according to Crispin Porter + Bogusky, the Miami-based agency that created the site – rose to between 15 and 20 million in just the first week. 'We sent out a couple of emails to test the site within the agency and with friends and it went bananas,' observed Andrew Keller, creative director at CPB. Within a week, websites that tracked which commands the chicken would and wouldn't obey had sprung up: sure proof that this is an example of an ad agency getting the viral recipe (excuse the pun) just right.

With a knowing nod to interactive webcam peepshow-style sites, the idea here is that you type in a command such as 'dance', and the chicken obeys you.

EXECUTIVE CREATIVE DIRECTOR
Alex Bogusky

CREATIVE DIRECTOR
Andrew Keller

ASSOCIATE CREATIVE DIRECTOR
Rob Reilly

ART DIRECTOR
Mark Taylor

COPYWRITER
Bob Cianfrone

INTERACTIVE CREATIVE
DIRECTOR
Jeff Benjamin

EXECUTIVE PRODUCERS
Rupert Samuel, David Rolfe

AGENCY PRODUCER
Terry Stavoe

INTERACTIVE PRODUCTION
COMPANY
The Barbarian Group

TITLE
Chicken Fight
CLIENT
Burger King
AGENCY
Crispin Porter + Bogusky

Chicken Fight, launched only a few months after Subservient Chicken, featured more men-dressed-as-chickens shenanigans from CPB for Burger King. Only this time there were two chickens, one representing the fast-food chain's TenderCrisp (TC) chicken sandwich, and the other Spicy TenderCrisp. Promotional posters put up in restaurants read: 'Burger King Presents Chicken Sandwich World Championship', and a TV spot raised public awareness of the event. And, yes, there was an actual event: two men dressed as chickens, battering each other in a 15-minute battle staged amid gladiatorial festivity in a caged arena at the Pico Rivera Sport arena outside Los Angeles.

★ BURGER KING® PRESENTS ★

CHICKEN SANDWICH

WORLD
★CHAMPIONSHIP★

"TC"   VS   **"Spicy"**

AKA **TENDERCRISP** Chicken   AKA Spicy **TENDERCRISP** Chicken

★ ★ ¡YOU DECIDE! ★ ★

CHICKENFIGHT.COM

An accompanying website, www.chickenfight.com, offered background information on the two opponents, such as the fact that Spicy (aka 'The Red Riot') hailed from New Mexico and was known for his ferocious kicking ability, and invited visitors to vote for their favourite bird/sandwich. So impressive was the hype around the event that intertops.com, one of the Internet's largest sports betting sites, accepted bets on the outcome.

There were also complaints about Burger King using the idea of cockfighting to promote its food. When the Humane Society of the United States called on the company to pull the 'chicken fight' ad because it made fun of the barbaric and widespread practice of cockfighting, Burger King issued the following disclaimer: 'No real chickens were harmed in the making of this advertising campaign. Burger King Corporation does not endorse or condone animal cruelty in any way, including chicken fighting. The chicken characters featured in this advertising campaign are just actors wearing a chicken costume.'

More than a million people visited the chickenfight.com site to register a vote for their favourite chicken. The event was televised and simultaneously webcast at http://msn.foxsports.com/chickenfight.

The Gold Bird TC vs. Red Hot Spicy.
Two chickens. One quest.
The Chicken Sandwich
World Championship.
See who wins. It's time to take sides.

PRODUCTION COMPANY
@radical.media,
Los Angeles

EDITING COMPANY
Cosmo Street,
Los Angeles

MUSIC COMPANY
Beacon Street Music

EXECUTIVE CREATIVE DIRECTOR
Alex Bogusky

CREATIVE DIRECTOR
Andrew Keller

ASSOCIATE CREATIVE DIRECTOR
Rob Reilly

ART DIRECTOR
James Dawson-Hollis

WRITER
Rob Strasberg

DIRECTOR
The Glue Society

INTERACTIVE CREATIVE
DIRECTOR
Jeff Benjamin

INTERACTIVE ART DIRECTOR
Michael Ferrare

EXECUTIVE AGENCY
PRODUCERS
Rupert Samuel,
David Rolfe

AGENCY PRODUCER
Corey Bartha

INTERACTIVE PRODUCER
Paul Sutton

DIRECTOR OF PHOTOGRAPHY
Igor Jadue-Lillo

EDITOR
Chan Hatcher

ASSISTANT EDITOR
Christjan Jordan

EXECUTIVE PRODUCER
Frank Scherma

MUSIC
Andrew Feltenstein,
John Nau

AGENCY MUSIC PRODUCER
Bill Meadows

MOTION GRAPHICS
COMPANY BRAND
New School

INTERACTIVE
DEVELOPMENT PARTNER
WDDG

INTERACTIVE PHOTOGRAPHER
Kyla Kuhner

PRINT PRODUCER
Eva Dimick

ART PRODUCER
Jessica Hoffman

ILLUSTRATORS
Mike Koelsch, James
Dawson-Hollis

AKESTAM.HOLST (Sweden) www.fabriken.akestamholst.se
ALT TERRAIN (USA) www.altterrain.com
AMV BBDO (UK) www.amvbbdo.com
BARTLE BOGLE HEGARTY (UK) www.bartleboglehegarty.com
CAKE (UK) www.cakegroup.com
COLE & WEBER / RED CELL (USA) www.coleweber.com
COLENSO BBDO (New Zealand) www.colensobbdo.co.nz
CONTRACT (India) www.contractadvertising.com
CRISPIN PORTER + BOGUSKY (USA) www.cpbgroup.com
CUNNING (UK) www.cunningwork.com
DAZED (USA) www.dazedfilmtv.com
DDB (Hong Kong) www.ddb.com
DDB LONDON (UK) www.ddblondon.com
DENTSU (Japan) www.dentsu.com/www.dentsu.co.jp
DIGIT (UK) www.digitlondon.com
FALLON (UK) www.fallon.co.uk
FCB SINGAPORE (Singapore) www.fcb.com
THE FISH CAN SING (UK) www.thefishcansing.com
HICKLIN SLADE AND PARTNERS (UK) www.hicklinslade.com
HIVE PARTNERS (UK) www.hivepartners.com
HOOPER GALTON (UK) www.hoopergalton.co.uk
JUNG VON MATT (Germany) www.jvm.de
JWT (Brazil/ Malaysia/ UK) www.jwt.com
KESSELSKRAMER (The Netherlands) www.kesselskramer.nl
LEO BURNETT (Spain/USA) www.leoburnett.com
M&C SAATCHI (UK) www.mcsaatchi.com
MAVERICK (Australia) www.mavcam.com.au
MICHAEL CONRAD & LEO BURNETT (Germany) www.leoburnett.de
MOTHER (UK) www.motherlondon.co.uk
NAGA DDB (Malaysia) www.ddb.com
NET#WORK BBDO (South Africa) www.bbdo.com
OGILVY & MATHER (Singapore) www.ogilvy.com
PPGH/JWT (The Netherlands) www.ppghjwt.nl
PUBLICIS (UK) www.publicis.co.uk
PUBLICIS MOJO (Australia) www.publicismojo.com.au
R/GA (USA) www.rga.com
RETHINK (Canada) www.rethinkadvertising.com
SAATCHI & SAATCHI (Singapore/Australia/USA/UK) www.saatchi.com
SPRINGER & JACOBY WERBUNG (Germany) www.sj.com
STRAWBERRYFROG (The Netherlands) www.strawberryfrog.com
TBWA\CHIAT\DAY (USA) www.tbwachiat.com
TBWA\PARIS (France) www.tbwa-france.com
TBWA\JAPAN (Japan) www.tbwajapan.co.jp
TBWA\LONDON (UK) www.tbwa.co.uk
TBWA\SINGAPORE (Singapore) www.tbwa.com
UNIVERSAL MCCANN (USA) www.universalmccann.com
WIEDEN + KENNEDY (USA) www.wk.com
Y&R (USA) www.yr.com/yr/

Get more people into Church is a brief that most creatives would baulk at. Not so, however at agency Jung von Matt. Creatives Joachim Silber and Paul Fleig decided that if the peop
manner of locations, turning more heads than a streaker at the vicar's tea party. Not only has it inspired poetry, you can even hire it for your wedding. In this amusing campaign for E
then paraded up and down the beach bearing the message: 'Homesick? We fly to the UK 77 times a week'. To celebrate B-movie star Godzilla's 50th anniversary, Sitges Sci-Fi & Fantas
A red carpet ran through the seaside town of Sitges, emerging from the sea to lead up the beach, on to the roads and directly to the festival's main venue. The idea, of course, was tha
another above a high bridge counselled the VIP monster to mind his head. To advertise the television show *CSI: Crime Scene Investigation*, Saatchi & Saatchi set up fictitious crime scenes in
of the show. My favourite is the blood-soaked suitcase sticking out of a locker. In this campaign for British Airways, M&C Saatchi brought various London landmarks to European ci
back of his director's-style chair bore the words: 'London is closer than you think'. In one Paris Metro station a poster was devised to create the illusion that a hole in the wall led to
London') appeared in Stockholm, and a poster in Copenhagen bearing the campaign slogan had sensors which were triggered by passers by and called out to them in uni
più vicina di quanto pensi'. Double-takes guaranteed… Fallon turned a section of London's Bank Underground station into a departure lounge to promote United Airlines: as peop
Sandberg to create over 150 painted views as if from an aeroplane window, which were placed along the adjacent tunnel to add to the aeronautical illusion. Ah, the Mini: it's famously
on several taxis to look like washing machines: real clothes, real water, real detergent, real suds, great use of media. A life-size model of the Volkswagen Polo Twist made entirely of ic
were used in a four-week national press advertisement. Carved from nine and a half tonnes of ice imported from Canada, the sculpture took three sculptors around 350 hours to crea
Philip Hughes, managing director of Ice Box (the company who created the sculpture) commented: 'We have worked on hundreds of projects for major brands throughout the UK
flyers that their luggage handling isn't perhaps as brutal as that of their competitors. Whether you could actually put two dozen eggs in the hold on one of their flights and still expe
provide comic relief towards the end of the flying experience, in a place guaranteed to be the focus of all passengers' attention. White vans bearing the advertising recruitment firm,
are therefore perfectly placed to recruit for them – so specifically targeting them in a way that advertising folk would acknowledge. A pick-up truck zooms past on the highway, pur
filled balloons attached by cords to the truck, which as they fly behind it create the illusion of three missiles in hot pursuit. This took Grand Prix in the Outdoor category at the Cannes
driverless as it drove around making deliveries. Conventional Impossible is Nothing is not. To raise awareness of this idea, before Vertical Football or Impossible Sprint (pages 154–
this stunt demonstrated it: strongmen pulled the buses, though members of the public were invited to have a go too. Not surprisingly, it attracted a fair bit of publicity in the process. I
containers – which, of course, symbolize global trade and are highly visible at ports, harbours and other busy trade centres. J-Wave is a Japanese radio station based in the imposing T
upper floors of the building, visible for miles around. In early October 2003, intrigued locals spotting the pulsating lights turned on their radios to find that the display was synchro
of the most memorable guerrilla campaigns of recent years to take place in London. A naked woman projected on to the Houses of Parliament makes a perfect recipe for media cove
poll in 1999. The woman projected, TV presenter Gail Porter, got a very respectable top ten rating reaching number eight. The Fish Can Sing called upon new media and interactiv
London's Design Museum for eight weeks in 2002. When passers by called one of several special numbers (printed on the outside of the tank in which the installation was housed),
price if they shop at IKEA and embrace IKEA's 'Go Cubic' concept. Eighteen living room installations appeared overnight in 12 different Dutch cities with IKEA shops. Each installati
a stir, the 'residents' at each of the installations encouraged passers by to 'steal' the furniture and take it home with them. JWT created the line 'Be proud of your loo' and placed this
details in the window of an estate agency is bound to intrigue even the least curious of people. On closer inspection, the accompanying info read thus: Knightsbridge, SW1. Large
loo. Continuing the theme, JWT also ran a classified ad using similar text in the 'Flats to let' section of the *Evening Standard* newspaper: advertising in forms and places that you'd least ex
public the lack of regulation governing the activities of British estate agents. BBC TV and radio, Channel 5, Sky News and national newspapers including the *Daily Mail*, *Daily Express*
crackdown on unscrupulous practices. *Which?* Director of Campaigns and Communications, Nick Stace explains: 'It's madness. I've had no training in the property market and I've i
campaign the government undertook to cut the proposed two-year wait before a full investigation into the state of the industry was carried out. The follow-up to the Vertical Foot
ropes, one per lane, to reach the top of the track as fast as possible, the winner of the final bagging $10,000. The stunt was picked up and reported on by news programme
turn leads to tr
breakfast.' Brea
idea of the year
elements that p

and rallied support to halt its release. Soon after this two more sites appeared online, apparently set up by gamers who disputed Beta-7's site, and soon the gaming community was
Project) and Chelsea Pictures to cast actors to play the main roles in the campaign, including Beta-7 himself. The actors played their roles 24/7 for the entire four-month period of th
officials doggedly denied the very existence of the game. But as early as the testing stage, shredded documents from Sega officials, apparently found in Sega offices bins, were re-as
which were subsequently used to 'prove' that Beta-7 had responded to an ad to become a games tester for Sega. The various sites continued blogging online, and the ongoing, lo
conventional about this advertising campaign, which took the Grand Clio award in the inaugural Content & Contact category in 2004. Jury chairman Nick Brien, then CEO of ArcW
in terms of both contact strategy and very challenging content. The campaign really was an experience and the agency went out of their way to completely fuse content and contac
marketing campaign conjured up by Chris Aldhous and Peter Hodgson of Publicis in response to client Hewlett Packard's request for a campaign targeting young graphic profess
young people to show their work'. Except that this gallery space would start off completely empty, apart from some large-format HP printers and projectors. Young designers, illus
which exhibitors and spectators alike would witness not only a selection of imagery by different artists, but also the HP equipment facilitating it all. 'We wanted to position HP as the
branch of the campaign, ads for some of the show's content – but made to look like typical Hollywood movie posters or art gallery ads – ran in magazine *Time Out*. So did the campaig
first digital films also arrived and we uploaded them to the projectors in the Film Bunker.' As art arrived at the gallery, a third phase of hypegallery.com went live. In this, the online co
4.5 million hits with 90,000 unique users from 142 different countries. 2,500 pieces of digital art were uploaded to the site. Back in Brick Lane, 1,193 artists submitted their wor
November 2004 and attracted 32,000 visitors. HYPE Moscow followed… The experience will travel to cities all over the world, encouraging and promoting the work of young ima
Beer was brewed in Seattle for some 180 years before the brand was bought out in the early 1990s. At this point the brewery at the gates of the city – a local landmark with its huge
brand's new owners wanted to reintroduce it to the city of its birth, but had neither a big enough budget for new TV commercials nor any loyalty among young beer drinkers upon
who had supposedly discovered a box of old Rainier beer commercials in an attic, and decided to champion Seattle's all-but-forgotten favourite beer of old. Rainier Vision (think *Wa*
and generally goofing around. The TV show developed a cult following, partly as a result of the feedback mechanisms built into the programme: viewers could phone Tim and Chuck
in-cheek Rainier trivia. It also directs viewers to the bars, stores and restaurants that gradually joined a burgeoning trend to restock Rainier beer across the city. Tim and Chuck becam
down and aired on network television and locally during sporting events and after game shows. A vintage-looking press kit was sent to local and national papers (one sold on eBay for
launched in April 2004, are invited to 'Get chicken the way you like it', as the chicken, or rather man dressed as a chicken, stares expectantly at the camera. With a knowing nod to inte
there are things that the chicken won't do – and he lets you know by approaching the camera with an offended look, wagging a scolding finger. Within the first 24 hours of going liv
out a couple of emails to test the site within the agency and with friends and it went bananas,' observed Andrew Keller, creative director at CPB. Within a week, websites that tracked w
after Subservient Chicken, featured more men-dressed-as-chickens shenanigans from CPB for Burger King. Only this time there were two chickens, one representing the fast-food
raised public awareness of the event. And, yes, there was an actual event: two men dressed as chickens, battering each other in a 15-minute battle staged amid gladiatorial festivity i
Red Riot') hailed from New Mexico and was known for his ferocious kicking ability, and invited visitors to vote for their favourite bird/sandwich. So impressive was the hype arc
promote its food. When the Humane Society of the United States called on the company to pull the 'chicken fight' ad because it made fun of the barbaric and widespread practice of co
in any way including chicken fighting. The chicken characters featured in this advertising campaign are just actors wearing a chicken costume.' In one 24-hour period in 2002,
OutdoorVision/ALTTERRAIN LLC. The butterflies formed a trail leading from Times Square, where MSN had a major billboard, through to Central Park where a promotional event
campaign, Microsoft formally apologized to the city of New York and agreed to stop the campaign and help the city clean it up. So was this an example of a guerrilla marketing ploy
and ruffling more than a few feathers, Microsoft had communicated not just to people on the streets of Manhattan but to a far larger audience. The campaign generated no fewer th
shaped outlines around them, with the simple line: 'Try K2r'. In Singapore, designated smoking areas often appear as yellow boxes outside office buildings. Agency Dentsu Young &
bearing the message 'Designated Smokers' Area'. Simple but poignant. The Women's Information Safe House (WISH) is a centre in Vancouver's Downtown Eastside district that caters
lifestyle. To raise awareness of the charitable organization's cause, agency Rethink left this cardboard cut-out of a woman, clearly intended to look like a prostitute, tied to a lamppos
and thoroughly wrecked, Rethink added a sign with the copy: 'No woman should be left out on the streets. Support our safe house for sex workers,' along with the number on whic
Various messages appeared on the body of the bins to highlight facts such as 'Polluted Water Kills 6,000 People a Day' and 'Over a Billion People Drink Worse'. Did you know that cat
Adshel's light (rigged up as a black light) came on, glowing hand-applied lettering spelled out this curious fact, with the strapline 'We can explain'. As part of the same campaign for S
the fact that some 300 cases of this bizarre occurrence have been reported. Every parent who does the school run past this fun installation by Energizer in Malaysia will doubtless be
campaign for Amnesty International to drive home the horror that in too many places in the world people are locked up in appalling conditions simply because their religious belie
beneath. Chalk 'goals' appeared on brick walls in Amsterdam during the spring of 1996, accompanied not by copy but by the familiar Nike 'swoosh'. Strategy director Matthijs de Jong
resources. With this initiative Nike promoted the "Just do it" spirit in a simple way. This idea was executed in 1996 when it was still uncommon to think in media other than posters,
York (in this case the Manhattan skyline) and which fused into something typically Tahitian. Here the illustration has been manufactured in metal and mounted on a brick wall. Mar
impressively as this campaign from BBDO's Johannesburg outpost. 35 huge artworks – essentially giant banners – by local 'street' artists were erected on the sides of buildings in do
but also recognized and supported it. The artworks are all still in place. This campaign was so successful that Net#work set up a new branch in Johannesburg called New#tork in or

to church, they'd bring the church to the people. Literally. Thus, the first ever fully portable and inflatable church was created. It has appeared on golf courses, airports, in car parks and all
designed to target sunbathing Brits, a stunt plane was employed to fly over the sea off Sydney's Bondi Beach, leaving a smoke trail that looked like rain falling from a cloud. A billboard truck
ecided to mark the occasion with this bizarre but intriguing campaign by Leo Burnett, Madrid. The aim was to draw attention to the Godzilla-themed events taking place during the festival.
lways emerges from the sea, would be given the red carpet treatment should he deign to make an appearance. Signs suspended high up in trees warned Godzilla to leave them alone, while
s such as public rest rooms, parking lots, public beaches and train stations. The scenes were all cordoned off with bright yellow police-style tape, which on closer inspection revealed details
sers by who stopped to look at the work of an artist who seemed to be drawing the Eiffel Tower would discover images of the Houses of Parliament and Big Ben on his sketch pad, while the
station beyond. Meanwhile, red pillar boxes emblazoned with the Swedish equivalent of the campaign's strapline, 'Ingen har fler avgångar till London', ('Nobody has more departures to
on voices . A Metro station in Milan was dressed to look like a London Underground station, while above ground in the city, black cabs drove around bearing the words 'Londra è
heck-in desk, about to enter a corridor of tunnel, they were handed leaflets and brochures by uniformed air stewards who welcomed them 'on board'. Fallon commissioned illustrator Erik
here it is packaged like a big toy to appeal to that part of potential customers that has never grown up. With great original thinking, agency PPGH/JWT in Amsterdam converted the hubcaps
tside the Saatchi Gallery on Belvedere Road in London in May 2004. The stunt by VW's agency DDB was to promote a free air-conditioning offer over the summer, and images of the ice car
mperatures of minus 10 degrees Celsius (14 degrees Fahrenheit) in a huge freezer. Once installed on Belvedere Road the ice car, all eight and a half tonnes of it, took just 12 hours to disappear.
inly for live communications and events. However, the Polo Twist is the largest project for a specific shoot and single piece of advertising.' A stunt by Virgin Atlantic to get the message over to
terms with fellow passengers after the baggage reclaim experience seems somewhat dubious... But that's precisely the point: Virgin Atlantic demonstrate they can wittily talk the talk and
mplete with radar-style dishes on their roofs – were parked outside the Sydney offices of the big networks. The idea being that FBI Recruitment know what's going on inside ad agencies and
pear to be three heat-seeking missiles. Not a scene from a James Bond movie, but a campaign for action movie specialist TV channel CH-9 by JWT Malaysia. The missiles are actually helium-
dvertising Festival in 2004. This caused quite a few double-takes. Inspired by the name of this kids' snack, the windows of the cab of the white delivery truck were doctored so that it appeared
WA\Japan produced the Impossible Bus Pull, featuring buses customized to include the line that is now synonymous with Adidas. Rather than describe the spirit of Impossible is Nothing,
unched this still topical campaign back in 2001. The idea is simple: Make Trade Fair and other slogans relevant to the core idea of promoting fair trade were stencilled on huge metal shipping
, the Roppongi Hills Mori Tower. Agency Dentsu came up with the idea of creating a fully functional graphic equalizer display using 300 green lights placed high up in windows over several
o J-Wave's live audio output. The display became a talking point in the city as photos and messages were sent between friends on mobile phones and posted on Internet blog sites. This is one
important 'talked about' factor. But what was the campaign for? Men's magazine *FHM* publishes a readers' poll of their 100 Sexiest Women each year: this stunt was to raise awareness of the
it to create the Digital Aquarium to help promote the aesthetics of Motorola's v70 model. An interactive exhibit made up of 150 suspended handsets, the Digital Aquarium stood outside
d vibrated in sequence, resembling a shoal of fish. This street campaign from Dutch agency StrawberryFrog was designed to demonstrate how people can maximize their space at a minimal
square metres (91 square feet) the size of an average parking space, and included a resident eating breakfast, reading the paper and chatting to passers by. And if that wasn't enough to cause
state agent's window – the idea being that the vendor is so proud of their toilet that they consider it the number one selling point of their property. Seeing a photo of just a toilet on property
Rimjet toilet. Extraordinary performance from a 3-inch flush valve. Silver fittings, anti-slam toilet seat & dual flush option. Price £350 pw. Tel: 0207 935 7712. Harpic. Be proud of your
04, *Which?*, the magazine of the British Consumers' Association, and agency Hicklin Slade & Partners set up Cheatem & Ripoff, a blatantly rogue estate agency designed to demonstrate to the
nes and *Financial Times* covered the stunt, and online coverage included BBC online and Guardian Unlimited. Essentially it threw down the gauntlet to the British government, demanding a
f the Estate Agents Act. But I can set up and sell homes. Dodgy practice has left the public exposed to the unchecked, often illegal whims of rogue estate agents for far too long.' Following the
kyo in 2003 (see pages 104–5), Impossible Sprint saw 100-metre sprint tracks appear on the sides of skyscrapers in Hong Kong and Shanghai. Competitors winched their way up
orld. Working hours in Hong Kong are long, with many people working a 55-hour week. This means that most professionals get less than the recommended eight hours of sleep, which in
McDonald's
r innovative
d interactive
s dangerous
ussion and much blogging on the subject. Was this games tester for real? Or was it some kind of marketing ploy? Wieden + Kennedy worked with Haxan Films (producers of *The Blair Witch*
swering posts on the blog, responding to emails and even being interviewed by the gaming press. Meanwhile, as controversy over the Beta-7 site raged within the gaming community, Sega
ographed and appeared online, so creating confusion and feeding both sides of the argument. Months before the campaign played out, the agency had even placed ads in local newspapers
opment of the campaign included viral videos, voicemails, posts at independent gaming sites, emails, TV commercials, small-space newspaper ads and flyers. There is absolutely nothing
go, commented: 'The gaming community is highly cynical and media savvy: they don't want to be marketed to. The smart thinking behind the launch of the game was fantastically executed
pulled it off brilliantly.' This campaign threw conventional approaches to advertising out of the window – and not just for the sake of doing something kooky. HYPE was a truly integrated
ead of producing a print or TV campaign, Aldhous and Hodgson kicked conventional approaches into touch, and instead proposed creating an art gallery – 'a space where we could enable
-makers would be encouraged to turn up at the gallery with their work, so that it could be hung or projected onto the blank walls. The result would be a constantly changing exhibition, at
able young creatives to get their work out,' comments Aldhous. HP would promise to credit and promote the work of young creatives through the exhibition and its marketing. In yet another
isely six o'clock on the evening of 22 January 2004, the doors of HYPE were thrown open to the public. 'That first evening about 120 artists turned up with their images,' recalls Aldhous. 'The
ble to wander round a virtual version of the gallery and check out the art that was being submitted. 'Over the next four weeks, HYPE spread around the world,' says Aldhous. 'The website had
he HYPE gallery. Of those, almost all of them returned to the venue at the close of the gallery to collect their prints, essentially HP print samples.' HYPE Paris opened in the Palais de Tokyo in
kers, while also offering a tangible demonstration of Hewlett Packard's products to that demographic, in a campaign that has become an aspirational piece of brand communication. Rainier
the roof – was closed, as production moved to California. The beer slowly disappeared from both store shelves and memories. Ten years later, following another change of ownership, the
. Agency Cole & Weber/Red Cell's solution was to create a multi-faceted campaign based around an 11-episode late-night TV programme featuring two young Seattle guys, Tim and Chuck,
beer instead of electric guitars) aired late on Saturday night/Sunday morning, and involved them showing vintage TV commercials from Rainier's heyday while discussing all things Rainier
ail messages or send emails via the Remember Rainier.com campaign website. The site carries the faux vintage look and feel of the TV show, and provides endless entertainment and tongue-
ies, and every weekend they were out promoting the show and talking with viewers and fans of their show in bars and at festivals and events. Three classic Rainier commercials were brushed
host of promotional materials, stickers, postcard flyers, T-shirts and key-chains helped the brand appeal to a 21–34-year-old demographic. Visitors to www.subservientchicken.com, which
peepshow-style sites, the idea here is that you type in a command such as 'dance,' and the chicken obeys you. Within limits. Not surprisingly, as this is after all a Burger King communication,
d up a staggering million hits, which – according to Crispin Porter + Bogusky, the Miami-based agency that created the site – rose to between 15 and 20 million in just the first week. 'We sent
s the chicken would and wouldn't obey had sprung up: sure proof that this is an example of an ad agency getting the viral recipe (excuse the pun) Chicken Fight, launched only a few months
Crisp (TC) chicken sandwich, and the other Spicy TenderCrisp. Promotional posters put up in restaurants read: 'Burger King Presents Chicken Sandwich World Championship', and a TV spot
at the Pico Rivera Sport arena outside Los Angeles. An accompanying website, www.chickenfight.com, offered background information on the two opponents, such as that Spicy (aka 'The
that intertops.com, one of the Internet's first and largest sports betting sites, accepted bets on the outcome. There were also complaints about Burger King using the idea of cockfighting to
urger King issued the following disclaimer: 'No real chickens were harmed in the making of this advertising campaign. Burger King Corporation does not endorse or condone animal cruelty
,000 butterfly stickers, some bearing the slogan 'It's Better with the Butterfly', appeared on buildings, windows and sidewalks in Manhattan, the work of guerrilla marketing specialists
ernet software package MSN8 was taking place. Advertising in this way is illegal in New York and so, on 26 October of that year, in response to a major public and municipal outcry against the
wrong? Not likely. The butterflies were Static-Cling (using static electricity as the sticking agent, not glue), so the decals were very easy to remove and left no residue. By bending a few rules
ticles around the world. This simple guerrilla campaign for France's most popular stain removing product, K2r, involved finding stains on pavements or streets and creating white, clothes-
ted an opportunity for their client, the Singapore Cancer Society, to remind smokers of the deadly effects of their stinky habit. Thus coffin-shaped yellow boxes were painted all over the city,
orking in the sex industry. Its goal is to increase the health, safety and well-being of women working in the sex trade in Vancouver and support women when they choose to exit that particular
er street. Over the course of several weeks, the cut-out was rained on, splashed with dirt from the road, and generally abused by both the elements and passers by. When it looked bedraggled
ISH. To promote World Water Day public rubbish bins in Sydney were dressed with appropriately proportioned straws, handles and even lemon slices to make them resemble drinking cups.
er black light? Canadian agency Rethink put this fact to the test in a bus shelter Adshel for client Science World: the resulting ad appeared as just a white poster by day; but by night, when the
Rethink left the supposed remains of a case of spontaneous human combustion – including a pile of ashes, a pair of shoes, the cuff of a shirt and a walking stick – in front of an ad spelling out
e with the little ones should they return from the shops with the 'wrong' brand of battery. Not so much an ad as a landmark, there's just no way you could miss this jolly battery man. A great
or opinions differ from those of the regime under which they live. The campaign consisted of pairs of model hands gripping the grille of street drains – as though a person were imprisoned
ency KesselsKramer explains the logic of the campaign: 'By drawing goals with chalk Nike wanted to inspire kids in the suburbs of Amsterdam to create their own football pitch with minimal
mmercials.' To advertise flights from NYC to Tahiti, Saatchi & Saatchi commissioned illustrator Dennis Clouse to create single-line drawings depicting images that were unmistakably of New
d brands around the world have used graffiti methods such as stencilling to bring their campaigns on to the street in an engaging way. Few, however, have invested in the culture of street art as
nnesburg in 2003 to promote the mobile phone network Cell C. Entitled For The City, the project demonstrated the idea that the network was not merely rooted in the culture of the locality,
work with a specifically African flavour, drawing on local street culture of arts and crafts previously unharnessed by advertising. This campaign dates from 2000. To encourage trafficwebsite